SIXTY YEARS OF
LEEDS BRADFORD AIRPORT

by

Alan Phillips

HUTTON PRESS
1994

Published by

The Hutton Press Ltd.,
130 Canada Drive, Cherry Burton, Beverley,
East Yorkshire HU17 7SB

Printed and bound by

Clifford Ward (Bridlington) Ltd.,
55 West Street, Bridlington,
East Yorkshire YO15 3DZ

ISBN 1 872167 64 0

CONTENTS

INTRODUCTION

The intention of this book is to trace the development of Yeadon aerodrome from its humble beginning in 1931 to the present day, but before one begins to look at the history of the airport, it is worth noting briefly the earlier events that took place in aviation in the area. Yorkshire has always attracted the imagination of the early aviators and it is certain that if it had not been for these early pioneers and enthusiasts one might not be so fortunate to have the present airport.

Today Leeds Bradford is the main airport for this part of the United Kingdom, but up to the finalisation of the present site, numerous landing fields of various types were situated around Leeds and Bradford. Finally in 1931 the present site at Yeadon was chosen, as it was considered to be of equal distance between both cities.

During its first sixty years, the airport has had a turbulent history from a general uncertainty to the present anti airport protesters. While other regional airports have enjoyed the blessing of the local community, Leeds Bradford has been less fortunate; every major expansion and application for extending operating hours has been greeted with hostility and ended up in long drawn out public inquiries. Most of the protesters' fears about noise pollution and possible devaluation of their properties are unfounded, as by today a new breed of quiet aircraft are in service with most airlines and there are hardly any signs in a drop in property value.

The airport has more or less achieved all its aims, even the twenty-four hour opening which everyone had fought hard to achieve. The licence was granted in January 1994, and at the time of writing, night flights have been arranged by the tour operators for the 1995 season.

Today the airport as well as attracting business and investment to the area is itself a major employer with a total of 1012 employed of which 169 are employed by the Airport Authority.

Leeds and Bradford has a catchment area of nearly five million people compared with either Newcastle or East Midlands whose catchment areas are around 2.5 million a piece, but both airports can boast of handling at least 1½ million passengers per year. However these two examples have nearly twice the number of holiday charter flights. One finds the situation in Yorkshire that holiday travellers prefer to travel to Manchester or even Gatwick rather than fly from their local airport. The reasons being choice of flights to various destinations from Leeds Bradford Airport are limited and those that do fly carry a hefty supplement.

Leeds Bradford Airport is undoubtedly the gateway to all that has made Yorkshire the largest county in England, as well as being one of the most famous world wide. Especially now as the U.K. is a member of the European Community it's more important than ever to the future development of the area. Today Leeds Bradford Airport is within a few hours of all the Community's major cities, and as a result has attracted new foreign industries and business to the area. Even as far back as 1935 during the first inaugural schedule flight, Major Ackroyd foresaw Yeadon as a centre of commercial flying in the North of England, bringing a deserved prosperity to the area.

The airport overlooks the valley of Wharfedale and Airedale, is within minutes of some of the most beautiful scenery in the British Isles. So one finds it serves all aspects of the community whether one is a businessman, holiday-maker or a sport supporter. Without the airport the area would be the poorer.

ACKNOWLEDGEMENTS

Grateful thanks are extended to the following for their valuable assistance and information.

Aer Lingus.
Air U.K.
British Aerospace — Brough.
British Aerospace — Woodford.
British Airways.
British Midland Airways.

Mr. F. L. Clements.
Dan Air.
Mr. C. Dennison, Airport Director (Former).
Mr. Andrew Hill.
Imperial War Museum.
Leeds Bradford Airport Ltd.
Leeds City Libraries (various branches).

R.A.F. Museum Hendon.
Reference Library — Bradford.
Reference Library — Leeds.
Mr. Rockcliffe.
Mr. Bill Savage, Airport Director (Present).

Bradford Telegraph & Argus.
Yorkshire Light Aircraft.
Yorkshire Post.

Also I would like to thank numerous individuals who contributed a wealth of information towards the book and a special thanks to Mr. Clifford Walker without whose assistance and knowledge the book would not have been possible.

Finally, my thanks are especially due to my wife Lyn, for her constant help with the typing and encouragement.

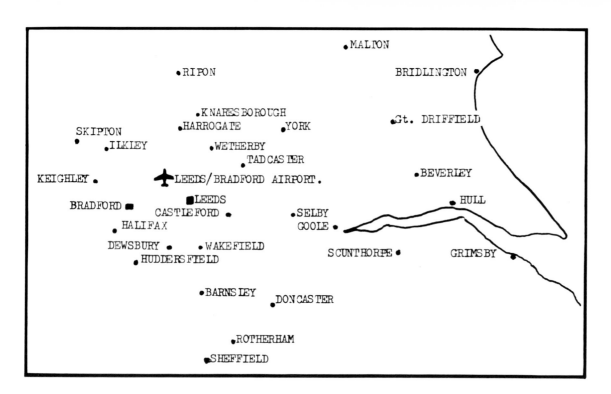

Map labels:
MALTON
RIPON
BRIDLINGTON
KNARESBOROUGH
HARROGATE
YORK
Gt. DRIFFIELD
SKIPTON
ILKLEY
WETHERBY
TADCASTER
KEIGHLEY
LEEDS/BRADFORD AIRPORT.
BEVERLEY
BRADFORD
LEEDS
CASTLEFORD
HULL
HALIFAX
SELBY
GOOLE
DEWSBURY
WAKEFIELD
SCUNTHORPE
GRIMSBY
HUDDERSFIELD
BARNSLEY
DONCASTER
ROTHERHAM
SHEFFIELD

*Leeds Bradford Airport Terminal
as it is today.*

THE EARLY AVIATORS

The first known Yorkshireman to be genuinely interested in flying was the Baronet Sir George Cayley of Brampton Hall, who during the early Nineteenth Century is known to have built a number of flying models in his private workshop. The drawings and plans still exist today and can be seen at the Science Museum. Sir George was not content with just building models, his ambition was to build a full size flying machine able to carry man. In 1804 he built a glider with a five foot wing span which is believed to be the first flying machine ever to fly in the UK. It took him another five years to build a full size prototype, complete with moveable tail surface. This was a remarkable achievement, but it was not until 1848 that the first person was to fly in one of Sir George's gliders.

That honour went to an unknown ten year old boy who is believed to be the son of one of Sir George's servants; the flight was just a short hop. The most important flight of all was done by John Appleby as the test pilot, who covered a distance of nearly 500 yards and has been regarded as the first human flight.

Sir George Cayley was a very remarkable man and no wonder he has become known as the "father of aviation".

The first ever records of any sort of flying in the Leeds area were in 1901 when the great showman Col. Samuel Franklin Cody, better known as Buffalo Bill, during a visit to Leeds demonstrated his war kites to government inspectors on Holbeck Moor.

In December 1903 in Kitty Wake South Carolina, in the United States, an event took place that would change the world, when Orville and Wilbur Wright constructed and flew a heavier than air machine. Soon aviators throughout the world and especially in Europe began to design and build their own flying machines and of course Yorkshire was not going to be left out.

Great interest arose in aviation, like the Doncaster Air Pageant from 15th to 23rd October 1909. This event was extremely important to the development of flying in the area as one will see later. The Pageant produced some notable flying and introduced some interesting flying machines like the Gnome powered Bleriot monoplane which had flown the channel some months earlier; the Farman Biplane and the famous Cody's Cathedral. The French designs won most of the events; as a result most of the British machines to fly later were based on these superb designs.

Bradford produced the area's first dare devil aviator namely Richard "Bobby" Allen who built a flying machine around his bicycle. He persuaded a balloonist Reuben Brumball to lift his flying machine by balloon; but at a height of just over six feet, the machine tipped over and Bobby Allen fell to the ground. Although he was not hurt, he decided to abandon the idea and disappeared from the flying scene.

The first conventional aeroplane in Bradford was a Bleriot Monoplane, bought by the Northern Aero Syndicate. After several months on view to the public, one of the owners John William House took the monoplane to a height of three feet but only managed a mere thirty yards.

With a growing interest in the area for flying, it was decided that a permanent aerodrome was needed. So in 1910 Rawdon Meadows was chosen as the site for the Airedale Aerodrome, which it was hoped would become a centre for aviators in the north. But it was short lived; due to lack of support, the idea was abandoned. Therefore with no proper aerodrome of any sort, the Northern Aero Syndicate moved its monoplane to Filey where it continued to fly until it crashed and the Syndicate was dissolved.

Also worth noting at the time was an event that took place in Halifax when the great British aviator Claude Graham White made several demonstration flights from the Halifax Zoo and Amusement Park in his Farman Biplane.

The most famous of all Yorkshire aviators was Leeds-born Robert Blackburn, whose aircraft company kept its connection with Yorkshire until being absorbed into the British Aerospace Company.

Robert was born in the city of Leeds on 26th March 1885, but while a student went to France to further his education and became interested in aviation. After returning, he persuaded his father to let him start his own aviation business, and in a basement of a clothing factory in Benson Street he began the first steps in what later became the famous Blackburn Aircraft Company.

At first progress was extremely slow. He was joined by Jack Rhodes, Harry Goodyear, and H. Wilkinson who together built their first aircraft. It was a biplane of Robert's own design. In April 1910 they transported the aircraft by road to Marske-by-the-Sea. The flights were rather disappointing as it hardly left the ground and when it did, only managed a few yards. Then on 24th May with Robert at the controls, it side slipped from a height of just three feet, but was extensively damaged.

Robert Blackburn did not give up. That particular design was dropped and within a few days he came up with another design, this time based on the French Antoinette monoplane which thrilled the crowds at Doncaster a year ealier. The only difference being Robert's monoplane was powered by the new Leeds built 7 cylinder Isaacson engines. The flights were made at Filey and were fairly successful. It was decided to start a production line, and new premises were acquired at the old Midland Railway stables on Balm Road.

The best of Blackburn design was to come; these were a range of the Mercury monoplanes. It was a two-seater powered by a 50 h.p. Isaacson engine; the fuselage was 33ft in length by a 38ft wing span and during the 1911 Olympia Air Show it was the centre piece on the Blackburn stand. Although it did not receive a single order, the sturdy and imaginative design did the company a world of good as one will see during the next few years. Robert continued to fly and develop the Mercury and in 1911 he entered two in the *Daily Mail* Circuit of Britain air race; but neither did well; one crashed on take off, while the other crashed at Luton on its first leg of the flight to Harrogate.

Blackburn was not put off by the poor performance of his monoplane, which most probably was not the aircraft's fault, rather the pilots who flew them. To be fair to all concerned, one must remember aviation was new, rule books and instruction books had not been written, but were written as they went along and a pilot regarded as experienced, perhaps had only an hour flying experience to his name.

In 1912 Blackburn Monoplane No.7 was completed and demonstration flights were given on Lofthouse Park Wakefield. Some passengers were taken up for a small fee which contributed towards the costs. Also during the year one saw Blackburn's most remarkable design of all, the E type monoplane, which was an all metal Military monoplane. Being of all metal, it was well in advance of its time, so extensive trials took place in the playing fields of Cockburn High School off the Dewsbury Road. It was found too low-powered and did not even get off the ground. The project was shelved.

For the next year or so Robert Blackburn continued to develop his Mercury monoplane, but in May 1914 the company was chosen to build the Farnborough designed BE 2C biplane, which became the mainstay of the Allied armies during the early war years.

As his factory at Balm Road could not cope with a large production line, a new factory had to be found. It was decided to take over the Olympia Works on Roundhay Road, which remained with Blackburn until they eventually moved to Brough near Hull.

Another Yorkshireman that contributed a great deal to the early flying in the area was Harold Blackburn of Carcroft Doncaster (no relation to Robert Blackburn). One event that is worth mentioning occurred during the Yorkshire Agriculture Show held at York 23rd, 24th, and 25th July 1913, when Harold delivered copies of the *Yorkshire Post* to the show ground each day.

Later in the year in October, Harold Blackburn entered the Yorkshire and Lancashire Air Race, which was organised by the *Yorkshire Evening Mail*. There were three participants from the two counties. Each had to carry fifty special editions of the *Evenings News*. After an extremely close and exciting race Harold Blackburn won the event. This remarkable aviator was again in the news, when on 22nd July 1914, he made one of the first recorded passenger flights in the United Kingdom. It was during a visit to the Yorkshire Show held that year in Bradford that he flew the then Lady Mayoress of Leeds from the city to the Bradford show ground.

When war broke out in 1914 Harold Blackburn joined the Royal Flying Corp and after a very distinguished flying career, retired from the Royal Air Force with the rank of a Wing Commander.

With the outbreak of war imminent, all pioneering flying ceased and efforts were put into the development of aircraft for military use.

Drawing of Sir George Cayley man carrying glider.

Blackburn Monoplane in flight.

*Robert Blackburn built his early
Monoplanes at his premises at Balm
Road prior to moving to Olympia
Works. Photograph shows the first
Mercury Monoplane flight over Filey
beach in 1911.*
Photograph courtesy of B. Ae.

*Before the outbreak of the First World
War Robert Blackburn built a military
version of his popular Mercury
Monoplane. Here a Renault powered
version is ready for a flight on the
beach at Filey in 1912.*
Photograph courtesy of Real Photos.

A modified Blackburn Mercury 'The White Falcon' was the personal Monoplane of William Rowland Ding, Blackburn's test pilot at Olympia Works. Photograph shows Ding at the controls taken at Soldiers Field, Roundhay, Leeds in October 1915. Photograph courtesy of B. Ae.

A Blackburn Mercury Monoplane of 1912 restored by the Shuttleworth Trust seen at Yeadon during a 1952 display.

11

THE FIRST WORLD WAR AND AFTER

In 1914, Europe erupted into a World War, the likes of which no one had ever seen before and it was not too long before it became evident that aircraft would be a vital factor in a battle. At first, these early flimsy flying machines were only used for observation; but as better and more modern designs became available, the aircraft was found to be a very formidable weapon of war.

Britain's total air strength in August 1914 was a pitiful sight of only 113 aircraft, most of which were taken over by the military from civilian use. It was decided as a matter of urgency, that only a few proven designs were to be built; therefore contracts were awarded to various companies throughout the country, not necessarily to firms with flying know how, but any company who had ample floor space.

In the Leeds and Bradford area, there were several firms involved with this task, the two main companies being the Blackburn Aircraft Co., as expected, and the Phoenix Dynamo Co., of Trafalgar Works, Thornbury. Christopher Pratt and Co., and March Jones and Cribb were also involved on a smaller scale.

Robert Blackburn received his first order in May 1914 for twelve BE 2C., but it did not take long before a follow on order came in for more BE 2C's. During 1916 the company was awarded a contract to build the Sopwith Baby which was one of the main seaplanes used by the Royal Naval Air Service. The seaplane was built at Olympia Works and shipped by road to Scalby Mills for test flying. Also by now Blackburn had begun to build hangarage at Brough, and a majority of the flights took place from their new base on the banks of the River Humber.

During these war years Robert Blackburn's imagination had not been idle. He designed and built the type L Floatplane. The first flight took place at Scalby Mills, where Blackburn had already built a wooden hangar. This floatplane was very similar to the early monoplane but was fitted with another wing and was powered by 130hp Canton — Unne 9 cylinder water-cooled radial engine. After a few flights, disaster struck. The floatplane was badly damaged and it was returned to Olympia Works, where it was totally rebuilt. It was taken over by the military, fitted with a single .303 inch Vickers machine gun and was used for coastal patrol, but eventually in 1925 it crashed at Speeton and was totally destroyed.

The most remarkable and the finest of all Robert Blackburn's designs to leave the Olympia Works was the Kangaroo. This was a twin-engineed bomber powered by two Rolls Royce Falcons 11 engines of 250hp each. Twenty in all were completed by January 1918, ten of which joined No.246 Squadron at Seaton Carew and were involved in convoy patrol just off the north east coast. The squadron with its Kangaroos attacked at least eleven U boats of which one was sunk and at least four damaged. At last Robert Blackburn had come up with a winner, but his final wartime design was for a torpedo bomber, the Blackbird, three of which served on Britain's first aircraft carrier HMS Argus.

With the move to the Olympia Works, Blackburn found they had an ideal airfield near by, namely part of Roundhay Park known as Soldiers Field and throughout their stay at Olympia Works all the test flying of land-based aircraft was done from this field.

The other local firm that was involved in aircraft production during the war years was the Phoenix Dynamo Co., of Trafalgar Works Thornbury, Bradford. In a way it was a very unlikely company to get involved with aircraft manufacturing. The company had been producing shells for the war effort since the early days of the war. Then due to its energetic manager a Mr. P. J. Pybus, the firm got involved in aircraft production and put in a tender for aircraft manufacturing. Phoenix's first contract was for twelve Short 184 seaplanes, which were flight-tested at Great Yarmouth and for a non-aircraft company, the quality of the seaplanes was of a very high standard, so much so that new orders soon followed for ten of the land-based versions of the 184. Phoenix also built the Maurice Farman Longhorn biplane in great numbers and these were regularly seen flying around Leeds and Bradford.

Phoenix's most enterprising and interesting aircraft built at Thornbury was the Felixstowe F2A seaplane. This large flying boat was transported by road, assembled at Blackburn's facilities at Brough and test-flown on the Humber.

The Sopwith Camel was another famous World War 1 aircraft manufactured at Leeds. Seventy-five of these superb fighters were built by March Jones and Cribb of York Road and served with both the Royal Flying Corp and the United States Air Service on the Western Front.

1916 was a crucial year of the War; the battlefields of Europe were in a stalemate situation — casualties were at an unacceptable level and the threat of Zeppelin raids from across the North Sea had become a reality, especially when York was bombed on 2nd and 3rd May. As the area was heavily involved in the war effort, supplying items ranging from aircraft and munitions to clothing, it was decided to provide the city and surrounding areas with air cover.

"B" Flight of 33 Squadron Royal Flying Corp which was on Home Defence duties was given the task of defending the area against this menace from across the sea. The squadron consisted of Avro 504's and BE 2C's. These were second-rate fighters which had been withdrawn from front line duties for training. They were lightly armed with a single .303 inch machine gun and it was doubtful if they would stand much of a chance against a Zeppelin's fire power armed with up to twenty machine guns of various calibre. But B Flight's presence around the cities gave some comfort to the inhabitants as well as deterring any further raids.

The City of Leeds was allocated three sites on its outskirts, namely Farsley, Middleton and Seacroft. All three sites were classed as primitive, as they consisted only of a landing area, some tented accommodation with no hangarage or permanent buildings. These fields came into existence in March 1916, but only remained operational until October the same year, when it was felt that the threat of air raids had ceased and other more permanent sites were found elsewhere in Yorkshire.

Farsley was just a grass strip situated a short distance in a westerly direction of the village, running north of what is known today as Dawson Corner, part of which is occupied by the ring road. Then it was just a grass field with only a few tents for accommodation and stores; but during its short time in existence it was kept fairly busy by Avro 504 and BE 2C of B Flight. As the field was restricted for any further development and with B Flight moving out, the landing strip was closed and the land returned to its original owners. The Farsley site was put forward as a possible location for a new municipal aerodrome some years later, but lost out to a new site at Yeadon.

Middleton, south of Leeds, was similarly occupied by B Flight, 33 Squadron R.F.C. It was mostly used as a night landing ground due to the flatness of the area. Again only tented accommodation existed and as the site saw only very little activity, was quickly abandoned. It is worth noting that the site was used for parachute training from stationary balloons during the latter part of the war.

The last of Leeds grass strips was at Seacroft covering the eastern secion, and like Middleton was also used as a night landing field, but again with no permanent facilities. Some activity did occur on the strip, but it was mostly used for training and the occasional patrol. During its eight months existence the Seacroft site was regularly visited by aircraft of 76 Squadron. Today nothing is left as a reminder that these three sites ever existed; where once Avro's and BE 2C's took off and landed, houses, factories, schools and roads are the new occupiers.

Other landing fields worth mentioning were situatd on the outer perimeter of the cities of Bradford and Leeds.

Dunkeswell was situated on the north side of Leeds, between the city and Harrogate just west of the A61 and north of the A659 roads. This consisted of a forty-acre grass landing ground, and again was occupied by Avro 504 and BE 2C of B Flight 33 Squadron. They were joined by Avro 504 of 76 Squadron quite often during their patrols of the Leeds area. Like the other landing fields, Dunkeswell only remained operational from March to October 1916.

A second field was at Cullingworth or Manywell Heights as it was more commonly known. It was situated just south of the village of Cullingworth, south of Keighley and west of Bradford, between the B6144 and the A629 roads. The landing strip was used by both No.33 and No.76 Squadrons and was operational a little longer then the rest, from 1916 to 1919. Again the site was classed as primitive with no permanent buildings, although Manywell Heights did have a wooden and canvas hangar for a while. Due to its vicinity, it was not regarded as an ideal site and was abandoned sometime after the end of the war. Today there is nothing left of the sites. Hedges have been erected where the grass strip once was and the land has been returned for farming.

Although some twelve miles outside Leeds, Sherburn was another airfield that came to life during the Great War. Actually it is the only site that has survived, but its appearance then was quite different to what one sees today. At the beginning, Sherburn was only a grass field with few permanent buildings, built mostly of wood; but as the site was not classed as a front line field, it became an acceptance park for the Royal Flying Corp. and later the R.A.F.

By 1918, the airfield covered an area of 177 acres with more permanent brick accommodations, as well as eight hangars and twenty-one storage sheds. Also Sherburn became involved in the building of warplanes, when Robert Blackburn who already had factories at Olympia Works and one being built at Brough, established a factory to produce the Blackburn Cuckoo torpedo bomber for the R.N.A.S. In all 132 of these bombers were built at Sherburn.

So one saw a number of landing strips appear around Leeds and Bradford area; but most of them disappeared as quickly as they came with the exception of Manywell Heights and Sherburn.

As the war came to an end, the Royal Air Force, as it had become known, had a surplus requirement of aircraft. It was decided to dispose of a great number of these. Most were broken up but others ended up in private hands and for the first time ever small air services began to appear all over the country. As well as surplus equipment, there were a large number of trained pilots, all looking for flying jobs. A few of these came to Yorkshire and

Short 184 sea planes were built by the Phoenix Dynamo Co. of Thornbury. Photo shows a Short 184 during trials with R.N.A.S.

The famous Sopwith Camel; seventy-five were built by March, Jones and Cribb of York Road, Leeds.

*An Avro 504 of 'B' Flight 33 Squadron
R.F.C. that were stationed at Farsley,
Middleton and Seacroft.*

*Blackburn Kangaroo – twenty were
built at the Olympia Works as patrol
bombers for the R.F.C. After the war,
three were converted as passenger
aircraft, two being used by North Sea
Aerial Navigation on services between
Roundhay Park Leeds and Heathrow.*
Photograph courtesy of Real Photos.

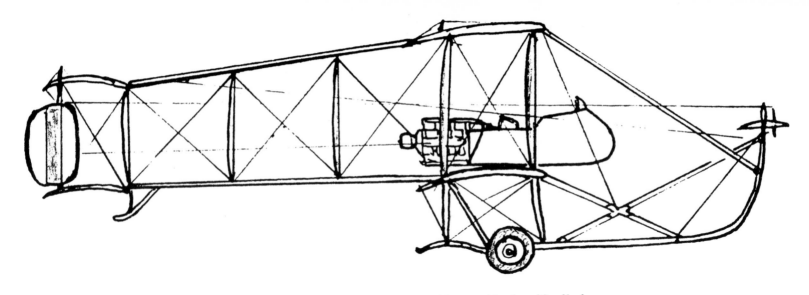

Phoenix built Farman Longhorns were a common sight around Leeds and Bradford area.

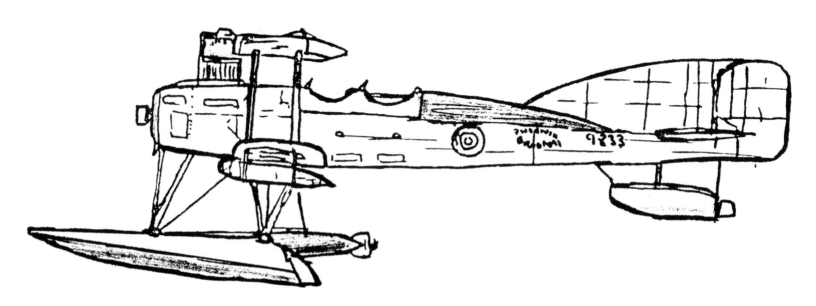

The Short 184 floatplanes were built by Phoenix.

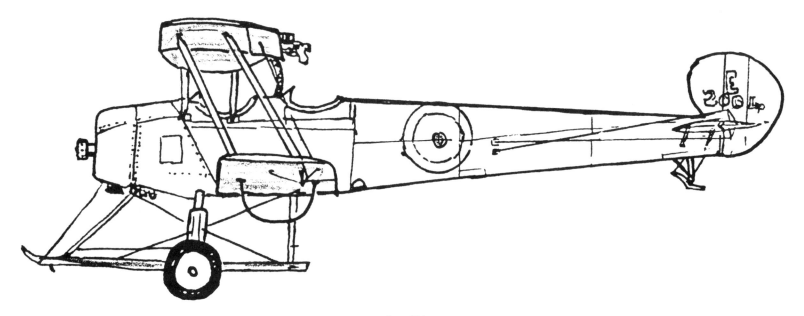

Avro 504

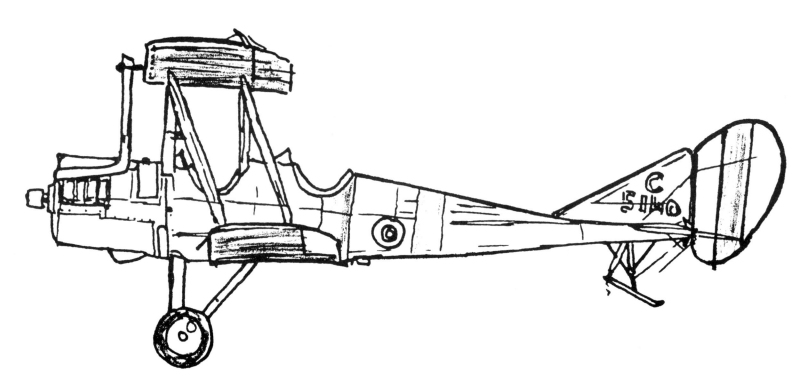

B.E. 2C.

especially to the Leeds area, as the city was fortunate to already have a landing field at Soldiers Field which by now had come to be known as Leeds Flying Field, run by Robert Blackburn whose factory was nearby.

The first of the services started in June 1919 when an ex R.A.F. Avro 504K was used in a daily parcel service to Scarborough. On a few occasions it is believed that it did carry the occasional passenger.

It was not until 30th September 1919 that the first schedule flight took place, linking Leeds with London. This service was operated by North Sea Aerial Navigation using two Blackburn Kangaroos, G-EAIT & G-EAKQ built some years earlier by Blackburn at Olympia Works. The flight was between Roundhay Park and Hounslow with a fare of £15.15s.0d single and £30. return; which compared with today's prices was extremely expensive and only attracted the well-to-do in the area. These early flights came about mostly as the result of a rail strike, when the Government took over most civil aircraft in the Kangaroo class for Mail flights. This particular mail flight was between London and Newcastle with a stop at Leeds.

The Kangaroo commercial aircraft was a converted bomber fitted with a glazed cabin for seven passengers and regarded as one of the most luxurious passenger aircraft of the time, considering most had an open cabin. Only three of these Blackburn bombers were converted and were acquired by Graham White Aviation. As a matter of interest the last Kangaroos were scrapped at Sherburn in 1927.

Also worth noting was another mail service operated on a regular basis between Hounslow and Doncaster with an occasional stop at Manywell Heights, but this was short lived and Manywell did not take any further part in flying as it was closed in 1919.

YEADON — THE BEGINNING. 1931-39

By the early 1930s the majority of towns and cities throughout the United Kingdom were either building or drawing up plans for municipal aerodromes. Not to be left out, it was felt that the cities of Leeds and Bradford needed a permanent site for a civil aerodrome. Up to then all flying had been from Soldiers Field, Roundhay Park. But as Blackburn had more or less completely moved out of Olympia Works, flying from the park had been drastically reduced. Anyhow this site was not considered really suitable for further development, and the area was returned to public use.

Various areas around Leeds and Bradford were considered including the old First World War landing field at Farsley extending to Dawson Corner and a completely new site at Whinmoor, and of course at Yeadon.

As it was such an important decision, Councils of both cities decided to obtain the expert advice of the famous aviator Sir Alan Cobham who had surveyed and developed a number of routes for Imperial Airways some years earlier. Sir Alan surveyed all the sites thoroughly from the air and on the ground and came to the conclusion the best site for an aerodrome would be at Whinmoor. This was situated on a plateau and had clear approaches on all sides.

The Farsley site was considered too restricted for any expansion as it was near the village of Farsley as well as being surrounded by hills.

The partly moorland and grassy field site at Yeadon was also not regarded as an ideal location, as there were too many drawbacks including its altitude and its proximity to high ground.

After several council meetings, it was finally decided that Yeadon would be the best choice as it was the same distance from both Leeds and Bradford.

As mentioned earlier the site consisted of grassy fields and moorland, just off what is now the A658 Leeds to Harrogate road. The nearest houses were over half a mile away on the Bradford to Harrogate road, so there were no complaints from the local residents.

In 1931 an area of sixty acres was established, comprising a landing area of approximately 300ft by 2100ft, which at the time was quite adequate for most types of aircraft in existence. The aerodrome was officially opened on 17th October 1931.

By October 1931 the Yorkshire Aeroplane Club had completely moved from Sherburn-in-Elmet to their new premises at the airport. As the club had considerable experience in aviation matters, it was asked to operate the new airport on behalf of the Joint Airport Committee which had been created by Leeds and Bradford Councils to oversee the new venture.

The earliest aircraft to use the aerodrome were various club types like the Cirrus Moth, the Gipsy Moth, later to be joined by the Puss and Leopard Moths and of course the renowned Tiger Moths, all of which were built by De Havilland who in the thirties was the main manufacturer of light aircraft.

The club chief-instructor and co-founder was the popular Captain H. V. Worrall D.S.C. Son of a missionary Rev. H. Worrall, he became interested in flying from an early age. He first flew in a Graham White Box Kite, but soon after joining the Royal Naval Air Service had the opportunity to fly more modern types like the Bleriot Monoplane and a Maurice Farman biplane, eventually progressing on to a BE 2C which became one of his favourite aircraft. It was not long before the dynamic H. V. Worrall was involved in finishing off the German battleship *The Goeben* that was grounded in the Dardanelles. For this exploit he was awarded the Distinguished Service Cross, and by the end of the war had received a bar to his D.S.C. and was awarded the French Croix de Guerre.

After the war, he became a test pilot for Blackburn at Brough, mostly test flying the Dart and the Kangaroo. Not content with such a peaceful occupation, in 1927 he joined Alan Cobham on one of his surveying trips around Africa. Eventually in January 1928, he joined the Yorkshire Aero Club and when the club moved to its new location at Yeadon became a legend. So great was his popularity and experience that during a Royal visit on 13th July 1931 Captain Worrall had the honour of piloting Prince George on a flight.

In June 1932 Alan Cobham made a return visit to Yeadon when he brought with him his famous flying circus. During his visit, as well as thrilling the crowd with an exciting flying display, he offered pleasure flights at five shillings a time in his Airspeed Ferry, which Captain Worrall had test flown from Sherburn, in an Avro 504 and the largest aircraft to land at the airport, a Handley Page W10. So impressed was Sir Alan by what had been achieved in the few years since he had surveyed the area in the late twenties that he arranged for one of Imperial Airways Handley Page commercial airliners G-EBBI *Prince Henry* to visit the aerodrome. One can imagine the great interest it created. As one onlooker remembered it was equivalent to the excitement that occurred when the Air France Concorde landed at the airport in 1986.

As passenger flying was intended from the beginning, it was decided to expand the aerodrome, and a strip of land about thirty-five acres was bought for this purpose. Also by now four steel and asbestos hangars were built, two just off the Harrogate road while the other two were next to White House Lane.

1934 saw the visit of two distinguished Austrian aviators, Prince Kinsky and Count Strahremberg. They were the guests of the Yorkshire Aeroplane Club. During their stay, the two gave a most remarkable display which was the talk of the club years afterwards. Both special guests thought very highly of the club and the aerodrome.

Up to now, most of the flying had been for pleasure and club flying, although some club members had taken passengers in their aircraft. It was not until 1935 that the first true airline service operated out of Yeadon. That honour went to North Eastern Airways, when on 8th April 1935, they introduced the London to Edinburgh service with stops at Yeadon (for Bradford and Leeds) and Newcastle using two brand new Airspeed Envoys. The inaugural flight was organised so that both, the southbound and the northbound aircraft met at Yeadon where a large crowd which included many prominent people from various parts of the West Riding had gathered.

Just before the final leg of their flights, both Envoys their silver colour glistening in the sunshine were christened Wharfedale (G-ADBB) and Tynedale (G-ADAZ) by Mrs. Eden on behalf of her husband Mr. Anthony Eden, the Lord Privy Seal who was ill at the time. Mrs. Eden smashed a bottle of wine on the nose of each airliner and wished God speed to the aircraft and all who travelled in them.

Passengers on the London flight were Lord Grimethorpe, Chairman North Eastern Airways, Mrs. Eden, the Lord Mayor and Lady Mayoress of Leeds — Alderman and Mrs. W. Hemingway, Alderman F. H. O'Donnell, Deputy Chairman of the Airport Committee, Major Cameron, Col. W. Boyle and a member of the press. While on the northbound flight to Newcastle and Edinburgh were Admiral Sir Cyril Fuller, Mr. R. H. S. Somerset, Managing Director of North Eastern Airways and Mr. C. Fullergill, a *Telegraph and Argus* reporter.

Total time for the flight between London and Edinburgh was 2hrs and 45min and from the capital city was only 70 mins. The price of the air ticket between London and Edinburgh was a mere £10, which worked out at 6d per mile. So proud was Lord Grimethorpe of the newly delivered, shining Envoys, that he stated in his speech that the first aim of the airline was reliability, second punctuality and the third bravery, meaning the aircraft would fly in all kinds of weather.

The Envoy was built by Airspeed which started manufacturing aircraft from an old garage at York. This little seven seater aircraft powered by two Armstrong Whitworth Cheetah VI engines of 315hp gave the aircraft the top speed of 210mph, although its cruising speed of brtween 170-180mph was more economical. North Eastern Airways ordered three aircraft, the third, G-ADBZ Swaledale was delivered a month later.

During the first month of operations, nearly six hundred passengers had flown, which was quite remarkable, but after a successful start interest wore off and as a result of insufficient demand, the service was terminated. A very sad ending to an enterprising scheme, but at least it was a beginning of schedule services from the aerodrome.

These early flights were not without incidents. On its inaugural flight, the southbound Envoy G-ADAZ carrying a party of dignitaries overshot a landing at Heston and ran into the boundary fence. Fortunately nobody was hurt and damage to the aircraft was superficial. Another mishap occurred in May when G-ADBZ Swaledale after taking off from Yeadon developed carburettor trouble near Ripon resulting in a belly landing in a cornfield. Once again no-one was injured, only shaken. The aircraft was soon repaired and it was not too long before it was airworthy once again.

In the same year 1935 Yeadon got a taste of its first fatal air crash. On 23rd March, a Miss Mary Clark of Leeds, a passenger in a Moth was killed when the aircraft struck some telephone wires during an approach to landing. Fortunately these fatal accidents were not common.

Seeing the potential of Yeadon as an access to the West Riding, the Blackpool and West Coast Air Service began a Blackpool to Yeadon service in June using either a De Havilland DH84 Dragon or a DH89 Rapide. The service was quite successful, and as a result other airlines began to get interested in using the aerodrome. In 1936 the Railway Air Service used the airport for a short time. Their D.H. Dragon Rapides, one being appropriately called the *Star of Yorkshire* (G-AEAL), provided daily flights in both directions between Yeadon and Manchester (Barton) with connecting flights to the Isle of Man. It was during the summer months that the Blackpool and West Coast Air service was absorbed into the growing Railway Air Service who took over all the airline routes including the Leeds to Blackpool. Manx Airways of the Railway Air Services took over all R.A.S. flights from Yeadon, and the aircraft began to appear in a new livery. By now the service was extended to Blackpool and the Isle of Man with a stop at Liverpool (Speke) on the morning's westbound flight. These early summer schedules were quite successful with a

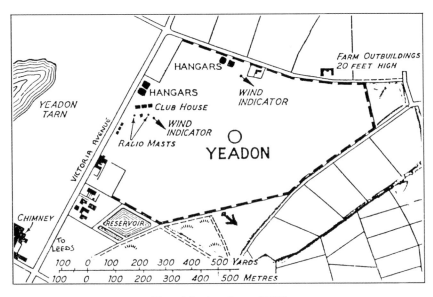

Plan of the Aerodrome (1933).

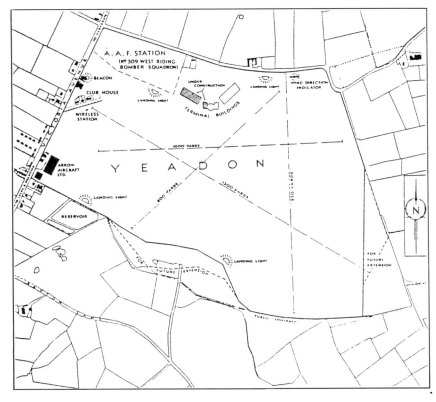

Plan of the Aerodrome two years later (1935).

high load factor, so much so that on a number of occasions a ten-seater four-engine DH86A Diane class, the largest aircraft in R.A.S. fleet was put on the route especially at weekends.

This service only lasted for a short period, but it was the beginning of the Railway Air Service association with Yeadon, which lasted until the outbreak of the Second World War.

It is worth noting, the R.A.S. contributed a great deal to the development of a regional commuter air service. Before the First World War, passenger flights on a commercial scale were unheard of. Therefore when hostilities ceased on 11th November 1918, civil flying was once again permitted, but it was not until the Air Navigation Act 1919 that real interest in commercial flying occurred and this only on a small scale.

It was not too long before the main railway companies saw the potential and perhaps future competition of commercial flying. At first it was regarded as providing an alternative, faster service to the railway, connecting the West and the Midlands with London, where passengers could get connecting flights to the Continent and beyond. So on 21st March the R.A.S. was registered as an air company with equal shares held by G.W.R., L.M.S., L.N.E.R., S.R. and Imperial Airways. Later smaller companies were merged for it to become a forerunner of the British European Airways in later years.

The mainstay of R.A.S. fleet was as mentioned earlier the De Havilland DH89 Dragon Rapide; this eight-seater, wood and fabric regional airliner was powered by two 200hp D.H. Gipsy Six engines. It had a cruising speed of 132mph with a range in excess of 500 miles. The first flight took place on 17th April 1934 and over 730 were built. In the thirties and forties the Rapide would be regarded as an equivalent to the Short 360 of today.

Within a mere five years Yeadon aerodrome had made its mark on civil aviation. It was even suggested it could be the "Croydon of the North". Traffic had increased and future prospects of the aerodrome looked good. In 1936 the field consisted of grass-covered surface like most civil aerodromes of the time, with four landing areas: a north — south of 700 yards, north east — south west of 800 yards, east — west of 1000 yards and a south east — north west of 750 yards. Four steel and asbestos hangars were available, which could cope with most repairs. Just off the Harrogate road stood the club house and office. Due to an increase in traffic and the introduction of an air service, it was decided to upgrade the aerodrome, and in October 1936 a short range radio became operational. Up to then pilots just landed and took off when they were ready to do so.

The following year the Railway Air Service continued to operate its service to Blackpool and the Isle of Man, but no new routes were added. Meanwhile the Yorkshire Aero Club under its energetic manager and secretary Capt. H. V. Worrall continued to expand; however the fees for a flying member had increased to £3.3s. entrance fee with £3.3s. annual subscription. Although the increase was substantial in 1930's terms, it did not deter any new members, and the club went from strength to strength.

Also in 1937 Air Taxi Service was formed at Yeadon. This new venture gave local businessmen and enthusiasts an opportunity to fly anywhere in the country in an "Air Taxi". Flights in a Leopard Moth cost 4d per mile per person, while it was only 3d per mile per person in the more comfortable two engine Short Scion.

Due to increase in traffic and rising operating costs, the airport management decided to increase the landing fees to one shilling for aircraft with weight up to 1500lbs. and three shillings between 3600 — 4500lbs.

Although Manx Airways had ceased operations in 1937, service to the Isle of Man was taken over by the Isle of Man Railway Air Service which was also a subsidiary of the Railway Air Service. This new airline consisted of eight DH89 Dragon Rapides of which G-AEAL *Star of Yorkshire* and G-AEAJ *Star of Lancashire* became regular visitors to the airport, throughout the latter part of the thirties.

On 16th September 1938 the Air Navigation (Licencing of Public Transport) order was passed, which meant that all airlines had to apply for licences to operate any air service from British airports as well as all routes. So this was to be the beginning of the present licencing system one has today. However Yeadon was only mentioned by two airlines, namely the Isle of Man Railway Air Service and the North Eastern Airways.

The total number of passengers handled by the airport in 1938 was 1,552, which was quite encouraging, but there was still room for improvement; but as early as 1938 it was felt that further development was required to attract new business.

Since 1919, carrying of mail by aircraft had grown considerably, especially so in the late twenties and thirties as Imperial Airways opened new routes to various destinations in the Commonwealth. North Eastern Airways received a contract from the Post Office to despatch mail from Perth (Scotland) to London, with pickup points at Newcastle, Yeadon and Doncaster. So on 3rd October 1938

the first mail flight took place. The service started from Perth using a DH Rapide, but due to high winds, an Airspeed Envoy (G-ADAX — Tynedale) piloted by F/O Gill continued the rest of the journey picking up mail and passengers at Yeadon and Doncaster. This mail service continued until 15th April 1939 when Yeadon and Doncaster were dropped from the run. Also it was the end of North Eastern's association with Yeadon, and Leeds and Bradford lost its air connection with both London and the North.

Services to the Isle of Man continued throughout the summer and the local Air Taxi still provided valuable service to the aerodrome and the community, filling in the gap left by North Eastern Airways.

With a general unrest throughout Europe and the threat of war inevitable, airlines became more cautious, passenger traffic dropped especially on flights to the Continent. Everyone seemed to be waiting for that fateful announcement.

On 3rd September 1939 the Air Navigation (Restriction in Time of War) Act became law; although it only prohibited civil flying in the east of England and east of Scotland, civil flying in the Leeds/Bradford area fell drastically. By now the Isle of Man air service had ceased and was not to resume again for another eight years. Yeadon was left only with the Air Taxi Service and the Yorkshire Aero Club whose activities had been reduced.

A typical 1938 advert for Yeadon Aerodrome.

North Eastern Envoy G-ADAZ
'Tynedale' taxi-ing.

Aerial view of Yeadon 1936.
Photograph courtesy of C. H. Wood.

*De Havilland DH 89 Dragon Rapide –
a mainstay of most airlines in the late
'Thirties and the post-war period.*

*Aircraft parked in front of the
Robin Hangar in 1936.*

The Bessoneaux type hangar at Yeadon 1937.

In 1936 Manx Airways, part of the Railway Air Service, took over the flights from Yeadon to the Isle of Man. Here DH 89 G-ASKE is being prepared for one such flight.
Photograph courtesy of MAP.

MILITARY PRESENCE — THE SECOND WORLD WAR AND AFTER

During the thirties there was a great deal of unrest throughout Europe. As a result one saw a gradual build up of Britain's armed forces especially the Royal Air Force. Airfields were upgraded with the building of new hangars, permanent brick built accommodation blocks replacing the old wooden huts. New runways were laid able to take the heaviest aircraft at the time, while the older ones were resurfaced. New, faster and heavier aircraft appeared on the scene; the old biplanes that were such a common sight in the twenties gave way to the streamline monoplanes that were making their maiden flights. Names that were to become very familiar in the years to come — the Hurricane and the Spitfire.

As a reserve force and a support to the Royal Air Force, the Royal Auxiliary Air Force was formed, mostly on civilian aerodromes throughout the country. The aim was to train pilots and other crew at weekends and during summer camps to fly and man modern equipment of the day. If the need arose these weekend pilots as they were known could be absorbed into R.A.F. squadrons.

It was not until 1936 that one saw the beginning of a military presence at Yeadon, although the occasional R.A.F. aircraft had landed before. On 10th February No.609 Squadron Royal Auxiliary Air Force was formed at the airfield and became known as the West Riding Squadron, which remained with it throughout. At first it was classed as a light bomber squadron equipped with the Hawker Hart to be replaced within a year by the Hind. Both aircraft were very similar in appearance and were powered by a single Rolls Royce Kestrel engine of 525hp (Hart). While the Hind's Kestrel gave 640hp, the speeds were very similar with the Hind only about 2mph faster.

Temporary hangars and accommodation for the squadron were constructed in the north east corner of the airfield, but these were replaced during the war by more permanent buildings as well as four new Bellman hangars.

By 1938, the war clouds had spread over the continent, and it was just a matter of time before Britain would be at war. Therefore plans were put in motion to take over all civil aerodromes for military use, of which Yeadon was going to be one.

Even the Yorkshire Aeroplane Club had formed a Civil Air Guard with a number of eager pilots, with their light aircraft ready to give assistance where possible. Flying training increased and even before the declaration of war, the Civil Air Guard was ready for action.

In December 1938, No.609, who by now had adopted the motto 'Tally Ho' was re-designated a fighter squadron like most of the the Auxiliary Air Force units. The Squadron's commanding officer was Sqd/Ldr. G. H. Ambler who remained with 609 until December 1939. The units continued flying their Hawker Hinds until 27th August 1939 when 609 began to receive their modern equipment, the new Vickers Supermarine Spitfire MK1, but before the Squadron could be fully re-equipped with this new fighter, 609 moved north to Catterick in September 1939 and was not to return to Yeadon until 1946.

The outbreak of war brought the requisition of all civil airports by the R.A.F. as expected. All private and civilian flying was suspended and all light aircraft came under the control of the military. Some civil flying did continue, but was under strict R.A.F. control.

At first, Yeadon came under the control of No.13 Group Fighter Command, but on 1st September became No.12 Group Fighter Command. Even with a change of group, not much really happened at the aerodrome. Not even a fighter aircraft came near the place. While, what was termed as the 'Phoney War' was taking place, it was decided to use the airfield as a scatter field for Whitleys of No.51 and 58 squadrons stationed at Driffield and Linton-on-Ouse, which at the time was under the control of 12 Group.

On 6th October 1940 No.4 Bomber Group Central Maintenance Organisation was formed at Yeadon. Its purpose was to carry out major overhauls for No.4 Group Bomber Command. At first the aircraft were Whitleys and Wellingtons, but they were gradually replaced by modern types like the Halifax which became a common sight at Yorkshire's airfields. Working in conjunction with the maintenance facility, No.4 Group Communication Flight was established at the airfield.

Neither Fighter nor Bomber Command had further need for the airfield; so on 17th March 1941 it was again transferred, this time to No.51 Group Flying Training Command. Before long No.20 Elementary Flying Training School (E.F.T.S.) was formed with fifty De Havilland DH 82 Tiger Moths, some of which had been requisitioned from civilian use from various parts of the country. Then within the next few months No.51 Group Communication Flight was formed, flying Rapides and Tiger Moths. 20 E.F.T.S was responsible for training thousands of pilots who proceeded to various establishments for further training and eventually to an operational training squadron.

In 1940 it was decided to build a shadow aircraft factory, on land taken over at the north end of the airfield, just off the A658 Harrogate road. When the airfield was finally taken over by the Ministry of Aircraft Productions (M.A.P.) the nearby shadow factory was handed over to the Avro Aircraft Company whose main factory was at Woodford, Manchester.

Most of the factory was underground and with a floor space of some 1,514,190 square feet, it was regarded as one of the largest units under one roof in Europe. The factory was set out as a single unit, divided into square sections with a roadway around each of its sides. Built of re-inforced concrete and bricks, it could withstand a fair amount of bombing if required. Thankfully it was never tested. The German bombers never found out its exact location. As well as making sure the building was of sound construction, M.A.P. went to great lengths to ensure the factory was fully camouflaged. The flat roof gave the impression of a flat countryside. It even had a farm house complete with some outhouses surrounded by a brick wall, with dummy animals about the farmyard — according to some local inhabitants they could not recall seeing any.

As there was so much pressure on Avro for their aircraft, it was found that the local area could not provide the larger number of workers required. Labour was drawn from both sides of the Pennines, from the North of England and from the south. At its peak around April 1944 the factory employed a total of nearly 11,000 workers ranging from skilled mechanics and technicians to cleaning staff, but only 47% of the total was male. Women of all ages, both single and married made up the majority.

The limited accommodation in the surrounding area proved to be a major problem to Avro and the Ministry. M.A.P. decided to construct three complete housing estates around the factory; in all there were nearly three hundred temporary accommodation blocks. A hostel was also built at nearby Horsforth, namely Greenbank Hostel which stood on the site where St. Margarets estate stands today. The hostel consisted of long rows of prefabricated buildings and was able to cater for over 700 of Avro's workforce. To cope with the task of finding accommodation, a special billeting officer was appointed, who managed to find lodgings in various parts of Leeds, Bradford, Wakefield and as far as areas around York. Some workers had a round trip of over 60 miles or so every day. To transport this work force to and from work was also a mammoth task and a fleet of buses was hired.

A thirty-foot metal causeway was built to connect the factory with the airfield, which is still there today to some extent, except now as a proper two lane roadway. The aircraft would be towed to the adjoining airfields where the engines and controls would be tested ready for their first flights by either Avro or R.A.F. test pilots. On many occasions one would see rows of various aircraft parked ready for distribution, which was the task of the Air Transport Auxiliary pilots, most of whom were women. The various aircraft would be flown to Maintenance Units throughout the U.K. for storage and acceptance, or sometimes flown direct to the squadrons themselves.

The first aircraft to be built at the shadow factory by Avro was the Armstrong Whitworth Albermere, a twin-engine reconnaissance bomber. But production was curtailed, since the Albermere was found to be unsuitable and did not go into full production. The few that were built were used for training and for glider towing.

In October 1940 Avro was given the task of building the single seater fighter — Hawker Tornado, which was to be a successor to the Hurricane. As Hawker were heavily involved with Hurricane production, Avro was asked to build and test-fly the new aircraft. The work was given to the Yeadon factory. Although the Tornado was designed by the successful team under Sir Sidney Camm, the aircraft was dogged with problems from the beginning, mostly with its powerplant, the new powerful Vulture engine. It was not too long before the project was cancelled and Sidney Camm and his team went on to develop and build the Typhoon and Tempest. By the autumn of 1941 Avro had completed a hundred sets and five complete aircraft which had been transported by road to Woodford, Manchester, where some experimental flying took place before the project was cancelled.

So far the Yeadon factory had only been involved with unsuccessful projects such as the Albermere and the Tornado. But as far back as 1935 the Avro design team had come up with a winner in the shape of Anson, and as the demand for the aircraft increased a second production line was started at the Yeadon factory.

The Anson or "Limping Annie" as it was affectionately known by the crews who flew her, was derived from the Avro 652, a civil transport aircraft which flew for the first time on 7th January 1935. The light bomber and reconnaissance version — 652A —first flew on 24th March 1935 in the capable hands of Capt. H. A. Brown. The Anson was a twin-engined low-wing monoplane powered by two Armstrong Siddeley Cheetah VI of 295hp each. The first squadron to receive the Anson was No.48 at Manston in 1936, but when war broke out there were twelve Coastal

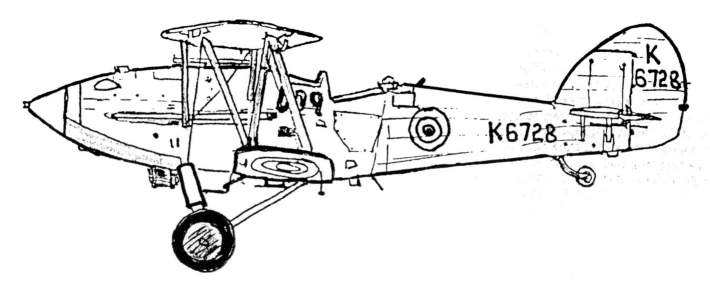

The Hawker Hind remained with No. 609 Squadron until September 1939.

Avro Anson I

Avro Lancaster B.I.

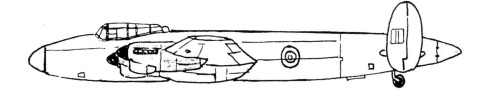

A civil version of the Lancaster bomber – the Lancastrian.

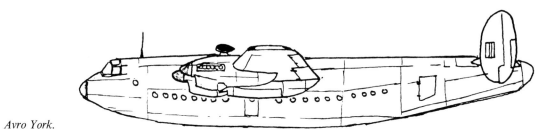

Avro York.

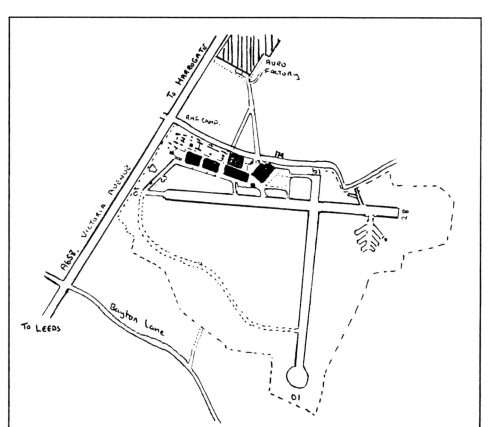

Plan of Yeadon airfield – 1944.

Command squadrons equipped with this remarkable aircraft. It continued to provide valuable service to R.A.F. Coastal Command for some years; but by 1941 its front-line days were numbered as more modern types became available. The Anson was then withdrawn from the front line duties to be used for training, light transport and communication duties.

Avro's Yeadon factory produced 3,881 Ansons of all types, of which 2,368 were flown direct from the airfield to their various destinations, while 1,513 were crated and transported by road. The actual breakdown of the different variants built at the factory was as follows — 1,026 were completed with the Bristol type dorsal turret (see photograph), 2,770 without turret and 85 for communication and light transport. Also it must be remembered that tons of spares were manufactured at Yeadon for distribution to M.U's and squadrons flying the Anson. The amount was roughly equivalent to another 800 completed aircraft. During 1943-44 a peak output of 130 aircraft a month came off Yeadon's production line — a magnificent achievement by its workforce.

During this peak production, large quantities of the Anson's engines, the Armstrong Siddeley Cheetah, were manufactured locally by Sir George Cohen and Sons of Stanningley, and transported by road to the aerodrome.

It was not too long before production was slowed down considerably, but the Anson continued to be built at the shadow factory well into the early fifties. As a great tribute to Yeadon and its factory, the last airworthy Anson WD413/G-BFIR, which had left the production line as a T21 in 1950, flew back to the airfield on 24th March 1985, to commemorate the aircraft's maiden flight fifty years earlier.

Meanwhile at Woodford, the Avro's design team had been busy with a heavy bomber for the R.A.F. This was eventually to be the now famous Lancaster. At the beginning, Avro's design was for a twin-engine bomber powered by the troublesome 24 cylinder X type Vulture engine and to be known as the Manchester. A few did see limited service with Bomber Command but proved to be a total disaster. Avro had to come up with a quick answer or the company would be left out of the bomber market. The answer of course was a four-engine bomber, to be powered by the reliable and trustworthy Merlin engines. The Lancaster was born.

The first Merlin-powered Lancaster L7257 flew on 31st October 1941 from Woodford and from that first flight everyone knew Avro had a winner on their hands. The Lancaster became the best heavy bomber of the war renowned when Wing/Cdr. Guy Gibson V.C. led No.617 Squadron to bomb the German dams. It was also fitted with the huge 22,000lb Grand Slam bomb to destroy Bielefeld Viaduct and underground U-boat pens.

Due to massive orders for the Lancaster, contracts were given out to other manufacturers in various parts of the country, and as the Anson production line had slowed down, the Yeadon factory became an obvious choice for the company's second production line. The first completed Lancaster to leave the factory was in April 1942. Surprisingly their Majesties, the King and Queen were visiting the factory at the time. As a marvellous gesture, His Majesty King George autographed Yeadon's first Lancaster as it left the production line.

For the next few years the sounds of Merlins were to become common around the Leeds and Bradford area; as one resident in Horsforth remarked, "they were proper engines not like the noisy ones of today".

A great number of Lancasters built at the shadow factory were for the famous Pathfinders Squadron. Secrecy was important when the aircraft were being fitted out with radar and electronic jamming devices; so much so that they were always guarded by armed R.A.F. personnel while parked at the airfield.

By the end of the war in Europe, production at Yeadon had reached an outstanding forty Lancasters a month and the total built by the shadow factory was 688 aircraft. As a matter of interest the airfield has not been as busy ever since. One eye-witness remarked the airfield was packed to its capacity with Lancaster and Ansons, as well as a collection of other various light aircraft, either waiting to be delivered or just parked.

During the war years, the general appearance of the airfield drastically changed from the grass aerodrome and a few buildings of 1939 to a fully equipped modern airfield of 1945. After the shadow factory was built the municipal hangar that had dominated the aerodrome in the 'thirties was found inadequate, and a new flight shed was built which could accommodate several Lancasters at one time. This shed was to remain part of the airport until the new terminal was constructed in 1982. Also two tarmac runways were constructed as well as parking aprons which were a major problem during these years.

When the war in Europe was finally over, there was still a need for a longer-range bomber in the Far East. Avro came up with a larger version of the Lancaster — this was to be the Lincoln. The first prototype PW 925 powered by four Rolls Royce Merlins 85 flew from Woodford on 9th June 1944. A later version of the Lincoln was to be powered by the more powerful Griffon engine. As for the new bomber, the Yeadon factory was only involved with the manufacture of sections which were transported to Woodford for final assembly. Only a few were completed at the shadow factory. The total number of Lincolns built by Avro was only 528 aircraft, a fraction of the number of Lancasters built.

It was not only warplanes that Yeadon became famous for. The factory was heavily involved with Avro's transport aircraft, which were to become common in the post-war period in British Civil aviation. These aircraft were the Lancastrian, a converted Lancaster bomber, and the true transport aircraft, the York, both of which were built at the Yeadon factory, and powered by the trusted and reliable Merlin engines.

The York first flew on 5th July 1942, but production was kept low-key as the bombers had priority. It was towards the end of the war when Yeadon became fully involved with its production. By 1948 the R.A.F. had nine squadrons equipped with Yorks which provided excellent service until being replaced by the Hastings. The York was also seen in the colours of various airlines including B.O.A.C., Dan-Air, Eagle Airways, Hunting Clan and Skyways — names that would be seen at the airport in years to come. Today the sole remaining York can be viewed in Dan-Air colours at the aircraft museum at Duxford.

On the other hand, the Lancastrian, being derived from the Lancaster bomber, was rather smaller with a capacity for thirteen passengers but was only meant as a stop-gap transport providing valuable service with the Royal Air Force and after the war with civilian operators like B.O.A.C., Skyways, Silver City, the British South American Airways and the Italian state owned airline, Alitalia.

By now the days of the shadow factory were over. The production rigs were dismantled and transported back to Avro's main factory at Woodford. Although the Anson was still produced at the factory in the early 'fifties, they too, came to a halt and aircraft production finally came to an end altogether.

It is worth noting that Avro employed several service and civilian test pilots, as all aircraft had to be fully flight-tested before being delivered to various destinations. One of these was the remarkable Yorkshire Aero Club instructor, Captain H. V. Worrall, who was mostly involved with flight testing of the Lancaster, for which he was awarded the M.B.E.

It was strange really that Yeadon airfield at the beginning of the war should get rejected by both Bomber and Fighter Command, but after some time of indecision, it finally became a supporting airfield for the nearby shadow factory. So Yeadon had a dull existence as a wartime airfield and never took part in any sort of military operations like other wartime airfields in Yorkshire, but Yeadon will be remembered for its aircraft factory producing the Anson and Lancaster, which like the Spitfire, helped to win the war. Without these factories and their work-

force building the aircraft — all other airfields and squadrons would be useless. Yeadon had a proud war record and played an extremely important role in the war effort.

As the war came to an end in both Europe and the Far East, the Auxiliary Air Force began to have its squadrons and equipment returned. No.609 was reformed on 31st July 1946, equipped by now with the latest night fighter version of the De Havilland Mosquito — the NF30 under the command of Sqd/Ldr. P. A. Womersley D.F.C. For the next few years the sweet sounds of Merlins returned to Yeadon, but it was only at weekends. The Mosquitoes would be flown out to Church Fenton on a Friday evening and return on a Sunday evening just to be stored in the hangars until the next time. During April 1948, No.609's Mosquitoes were replaced by Vickers Supermarine Spitfire LF 16e, a low altitude fighter bomber version of the Spitfire powered by a Packard Merlin engine.

On 1st September 1948 the Spitfires were joined by Austers of No.1964 A.O.P. Flight 664 Squadron which had been formed at Yeadon. The flight was kept busy working in co-operation with the army garrison at Catterick. The Auster became a familiar sight at the airport, together with other light aircraft that were privately owned.

The 'fifties brought the end of No.609's association with Yeadon, when in October the squadron moved to Church Fenton where they remained until their disbandment in 1957. While at Church Fenton, in 1951, No.609 received its first jet equipment in the shape of the Gloster Meteor F8. It only left the Austers based at Yeadon, although there was the occasional visit by other military aircraft, mainly communication types. Finally in February 1953, No.1964 flight moved to Rufforth, leaving Yeadon without any sort of military aircraft and for the next two years it was only used for diversion, which rarely occurred. One might say that the airfield was put on care and maintenance until 1954 when the Austers of 1964 Flight returned once more, but this time they remained until being disbanded on 10th March 1957. The same year No.609, now under the command of Sqd/Ldr. David Shaw, returned to Yeadon, but only to be disbanded. The Squadron put on a fly past in their Meteors, followed by an official ceremony attended by both R.A.F. and civil dignitaries. So with the disbandment of 609, Yeadon saw the end of its association with the Royal Air Force, as soon afterwards the small camp was demolished and during rebuilding in later years the Bellman hangars disappeared. As for the shadow factory, which is still there, the camouflage had given way to a more reasonable decor and it is now occupied by a container truck operator and a light engineering firm.

During the 'fifties and early 'sixties S.S.A.F.A. (Soldiers, Sailors and Airmen's Families Association) held their annual air displays at Yeadon. The first display took place on Whit Monday 1952 which proved to be an outstanding success, attracting a crowd of nearly 100,000 from all parts of Yorkshire and Lancashire. The vast crowds were thrilled by all types of aircraft ranging from a spectacular display by M. Nicole in his Bucker Jungmann, to a fly past by R.A.F. Canberras and U.S.A.F. F86 Sabre. There were the ever-popular rescue demonstrations by a Royal Navy Dragonfly helicopter as well as an exciting display by the Avro Autogyro. Static displays included aircraft like the Oxford, Spitfire, Dakota and various light aircraft; no wonder it was classed as one of the best displays ever seen. As the first display was so successful, it became a regular event, which attracted a large crowd each year all eager to see new aircraft of the day, like the Hunter and Javelin. Contributions also came from the U.S.A.F., when a Boeing B29K tanker version of the B29 bomber refuelled a Super Sabre, Voodoo and the twin-engine jet bomber the B66 Destroyer in mid-air over the airport.

By the early 'sixties, the airport was getting busier with civil flying, and in 1962 one witnessed the last S.S.A.F.A. displays at Yeadon. Thereafter the displays were to take place at Church Fenton where they still do. This last display at Yeadon attracted thousands of spectators. The flying display was as magnificent, especially the superb flying of the Jet Provost display team of the Central Flying School. Also for the first time the crowds saw the heaviest aircraft to land at Yeadon, the Blackburn Beverley. So 1962 was the last time the airfield vibrated to the sounds and cheers of the public air display.

Thankfully accidents were not too common at Yeadon. There were of course the usual slight mishaps, like collapsed under-carriage or the occasional engine failure. It was usually visiting aircraft or pilots not familiar with the airfield approaches and surrounding areas who were mostly victims. Also the airfield suffered from severe cross-winds and bad visibility which was another contribution to these accidents. One fatal accident did occur in June 1940 when a Hawker Hurricane of 87 Squadron stationed at Church Fenton crashed killing its pilot, Flying Officer Dunn. Several others both major and minor accidents happened, mostly during an aircraft's approach, a good example being on 9th August 1948, when a Spitfire LF16 of 609 Squadron, on its final approach struck an obstruction. Thankfully the pilot emerged from the aircraft only slightly hurt, but the Spitfire was badly damaged, so much so it was later "struck off charge".

Military presence has not completely ceased at Leeds Bradford, especially since the runway has been extended. In recent years one has been fortunate to witness several of the R.A.F. aircraft at the airport. Types seen are mostly transport aircraft like the Lockhead Hercules and Tristar and the B.Ae. VC10 used on trooping flights, a far cry from Lancastrians, Yorks and Dakotas of years gone by. Occasionally fighters and bombers have used its runways including the Phantoms, Canberras and Hunters and recently Harriers and Sea Harriers.

As recently as the summer of 1988 L.B.A. was fortunate to be visited by the R.A.F. last operational piston engine aircraft, the Griffon-powered Avro Shackleton, on a training flight. The strange irony of it was the aircraft seemed to be making a curiosity visit to the place where its predecessors were built, as the Shackleton was derived from the Lincoln and Lancaster.

For a number of years B.Ae 748, B.Ae 146 and Westland Wessex of the Queen's Flight have been regular visitors at the airport and no doubt one will continue to see them for a long time to come.

Thus there has been a full military presence at Yeadon roughly from 1936 to 1957, with just a minor presence since. It is doubtful if there will be a full R.A.F. presence again, unless there is a threat of war, but no doubt visiting R.A.F. aircraft of every size and description will continue to be seen.

*Hawker Hart which served with No. 609
Squadron at Yeadon in 1936.*
Photograph courtesy of RAF Museum.

*Hawker Tornado was built by Avro at the
Shadow Factory.*

*Avro Anson – 3,881 were built
by Avro at Yeadon.*
Photograph courtesy of
British Aerospace.

*Avro Anson T21 was the last variant
to be built at Yeadon.*
Photograph courtesy of MAP.

*Avro Lancaster B1 ready for delivery
in No. 103 Squadron colours.*
Photograph courtesy of B. Ae.

*Successor to the Lancaster was the
Avro Lincoln; sections were built at
the Shadow Factory.*
Photograph courtesy of B. Ae.

The Lancastrian was a transport version of the famous Lancaster.

Avro York – the first true Military transport aircraft built for the R.A.F.

Austers A.O.P.6 of 1964 A.O.P. Flights were based at Yeadon in the late 'Forties and early 'Fifties. Photograph courtesy of MAP.

No. 609 Squadron Spitfire LF16 with a collapsed undercarriage.

Spitfire LF16 of 609 Squadron parked outside one of Yeadon's Bellman Hangars.

A Fleet Air Arm Dragonfly search and rescue helicopter taken during S.S.A.F.A. air display on Whit Monday 1952.

A Spitfire VB belonging to the Battle of Britain flight at Yeadon during the 1959 annual air display. Photograph courtesy of MAP.

No. 609 Squadron Meteor during a brief visit in 1957.

Westland Dragonfly of the Central Flying School.
Photograph courtesy of MAP.

The heaviest aircraft to land at Yeadon – the Blackburn Beverley during an air display in 1962.

*Today's equivalent of the
Beverley – an R.A.F.
Lockheed Hercules.*

*R.A.F. B. Ae VC10 of No. 10 Squadron
is a regular visitor to the airport.*

The old Avro Shadow factory as it is today.

Taken in September 1946 'Chasers' at the Avro factory posing in front of an Anson that had just come off the production line.

42

THE POST WAR PERIOD 1947-1959

It was not until 1st January 1947 that the Ministry of Aircraft Production returned the airfield to civil use, although a military presence continued at Yeadon for some years yet.

By now the last of the warplanes had left the production line at Avro's shadow factory. The mass of imported labour had returned to their home towns and villages, and the local workers were employed elsewhere or were on the dole queue. Avro still kept a skeleton staff at the factory, but only a trickle of Ansons came off the production line.

Ownership was given to the Ministry of Civil Aviation as in the case of most aerodromes in the country after the war; they became responsible for the day to day running of the airfield, from its maintenance to the emergency service cover. Civilian flying was encouraged to return to normal, at least to pre-war times, and within a few months the Lancashire Aircraft Corporation had been given authorisation to restart club flying, but as yet there were no signs of any of the pre-war schedule services restarting. L.A.C. saw an opportunity to begin a summer service to the Isle of Man using a newly acquired DH. Rapide and an Airspeed Consul commercial airliners. At first traffic was rather slow, but as the summer months went by passengers increased and L.A.C. became very confident with their new service. Most of the passengers were usually the well-to-do of the area, but on one occasion a prominent mill-owner recalled seeing some of his own mill workers on the same flight.

Progress was also slow the following year. The Lancashire Aircraft Corporation still used the airfield with its few summer schedule services and the occasional special charters, but like the rest of the country civil aviation was rather slow in returning even to its pre-war popularity.

On the military side, Spitfires had replaced the Mosquitoes of 609 Squadron, and in September 1949 No.1964 Flight of 664 Squadron was formed at Yeadon equipped with Austers A.O.P. aircraft.

So the year ended with no airlines taking any interest in developing any routes from the airport. The Lancashire Aircraft Corporation was quite content with its summer only flights to the Isle of Man and was not prepared to invest in another route.

No.609 Squadron moved completely to Church Fenton in October 1950. The L.A.C. services had been drastically reduced and private flying was on a low key. Many local residents at the time thought the airfield had completely closed. A typical example of recorded aircraft movement in July 1950, which was classed as a busy month, was 300 transport aircraft and 1,047 other types like pleasure flying as well as military. Passengers handled by the airport totalled 906, but there was no freight handled at all.

The years that followed were even worse, considering that the majority of municipal airports were growing and developing all the time attracting new business and new routes. Even the summer scheduled flights ceased and as for the larger airlines like British European Airways — Yeadon did not interest them in the least.

February 1953 saw the Ministry of Civil Aviation pulling out of Yeadon handing the aerodrome back to its previous owners — Leeds and Bradford Councils, who without delay appointed Yeadon Aviation to assume control. Within a short while private flying resumed, but there were still no signs of any airline taking an interest in developing schedule air services from the airport. Once again in a matter of a few years doubt arose about Yeadon's future. If it had not been for Yeadon Aviation with its continued persistence and enthusiasm, plus full support of the Councils, the airport would have closed. Civil flying gradually returned, and more privately owned light aircraft became based at the airport. A few more charter flights appeared and most important of all some airlines began talking terms about operating out of Yeadon. 1954 also saw the return of the Austers of 1964 Flight, which a year earlier had moved to Rufforth, as well as the formation of the Leeds University Air Squadron equipped with D.H.C. Chipmunks, which became a familiar sight at the weekends.

For some years the Isle of Man had been a favourite holiday haunt for the inhabitants of West Yorkshire, but with the disappearance of the Railway Air Service, it was difficult getting an airline interested in the route. In the Autumn of 1955 Yeadon Aviation acquired a DH Rapide and began seasonal flights to the island, which became extremely popular.

Towards the end of 1955 and the beginning of 1956 a new airline began to take a keen interest in Yeadon and especially the north of England. This was B.K.S. Air Transport, a name that would become as familiar to air travellers and airport staff as Air U.K. is today. For the next year or so B.K.S. built up a network of scheduled services from Yeadon to various parts of the U.K. These were either daily or weekday flights to destinations like Belfast, Southend, Jersey and the Isle of Man more or less taking over the route from Yeadon Aviation, and for the first time, regular scheduled weekly flights to the continent — to Dusseldorf and

Ostend. Pleased with the response to these early air links, B.K.S. added daily services to Edinburgh, Glasgow and London (Heathrow), but the latter was withdrawn in October 1956 due to poor support. It seemed that Yorkshire folk did not care much about the capital city.

The majority of these flights were flown by the Douglas Commercial airliner, the DC 3 Dakota, or its military equivalent the C 47.

After the war the Douglas C 47 Dakota became the mainstay of most airlines, large or small. Over 10,000 of the type were built for the Allied forces in Europe and the Far East to be used as troop carriers, cargo aircraft and glider tugs. When the war ended a large number were converted for civilian use. The Dakota as it was christened by the R.A.F., and the name adopted by all the Allied forces became the workhorse of the services. This 27 seater aircraft was powered by two 1200hp Pratt & Whitney Twin Wasps which gave a range of 2,000 miles at 227 mph, and was ample for most airline needs. Strangely this workhorse of the Allied Air Forces began life as a commercial airliner but in the 'fifties came into its own when surplus aircraft were made available for airline use, providing then a reliable, sturdy and economical airliner at a reasonable cost.

With the beginning of continental flights as well as those to the Channel Islands, Her Majesty's Customs' facilities were instituted at the airport in 1956 and one could say Yeadon was on the road to becoming an International airport.

For the next few years B.K.S. became the main operator at Yeadon providing some internal schedule flights, but mostly summer flights. Up to now B.K.S. had all its own way without any competition. But on 21st May 1957 a new airline to Yorkshire, Silver City Airways with its Douglas DC 3 and later Bristol Wayfarer, began charter flights to the Isle of Man organised by the Lancashire Aircraft Corporation, who by now had got involved with the organisation of the travel industry rather than the actual flying. These seasonal flights, with a return fare of £6.19.6d, proved quite attractive to many a holiday-maker, and most flights through the summer were at least 80% full.

The first time Silver City used their Bristol Wayfarer it caused quite some excitement and curiosity, just as when Alan Cobham landed a Handley Page Prince Henry in the 'Thirties. The Wayfarer, although built for air transporting bulky cargo and cars, was converted to carry additional passengers by installing a passenger module in the cargo hold, but due to the excessive noise of its Bristol Hercules, the Wayfarer was not regarded as a popular airliner with its passengers.

By the end of 1957 the Lancashire Aircraft Corporation vanished from the scene, swallowed up by the up-and-coming Silver City Airways who had risen from rags to riches in a very short time.

With a general increase in traffic, as well as having several major airlines using the airport, Yeadon Aviation foresaw the coming of larger and heavier aircraft especially the new turbo props that were replacing the piston engine aircraft on most routes in the U.K., and perhaps in the not too distant future the true jet airliners. In 1958 they decided to resurface the two original runways 10/28 and 1/19 which had been constructed during the war, bringing them up to a reasonable standard to operate the new aircraft, but they were still insufficient for future developments.

On the 1st January 1959 there was another change in the airport administration. This time the Leeds/Bradford Airport Committee assumed responsibility for running the airport and on 8th January Yeadon aerodrome officially became Leeds Bradford Airport. As Mr. G. P. Sellers was already manager it was obvious he would become the first Airport Director or Airport Commandant as the post was then known. When Mr. Sellers joined Yeadon Aviation he was no stranger to the aviation scene as he had already had a distinguished war record serving as aircrew with R.A.F. Bomber Command. During his twenty-one years as Airport Director, he saw considerable change in the airport appearance and operations and was also involved with most of the planning and redevelopment one sees today.

Another personality that has contributed a great deal to the development of the airport was its Admin. Officer Mr. Clifford Walker, who was involved with the airport handbook throughout most of the 'Sixties and 'Seventies. Clifford Walker's love of aircraft and aviation goes back to his school days, when at the age of eight he became obsessed with a Sopwith Camel exhibited outside a cinema publicising the film 'Hellraisers'. Between 1940-1946 he served in the Royal Air Force as a Flight Mechanic, serving abroad in North Africa, Sicily and Italy, working on Spitfires of 87 and 76 Squadrons and later with Liberators MK8 in Egypt, India and South Africa. After leaving the R.A.F. he worked in light engineering until 1961 when he joined the staff at the airport as an Assistant Admin. Officer, then promoted to Admin. Officer in 1967. He and G. P. Sellers became an efficient team at the airport. Under the new administration, vast improvements took place, bringing it up to higher standards.

A new permanent airfield lighting system was installed as was a new runway and approach lighting on the main runway 10/28, which was long overdue. Aircraft parking had always been a

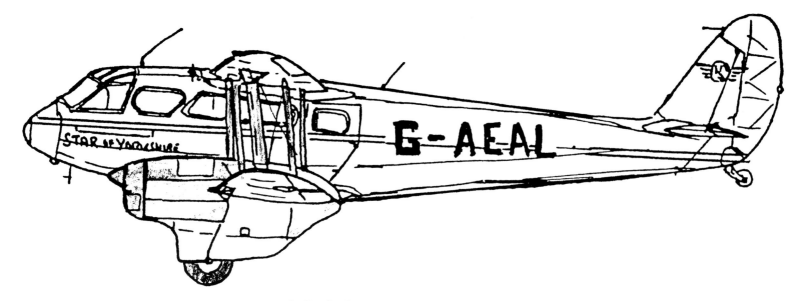

De Havilland DH89 Rapide – Railway Air Service.

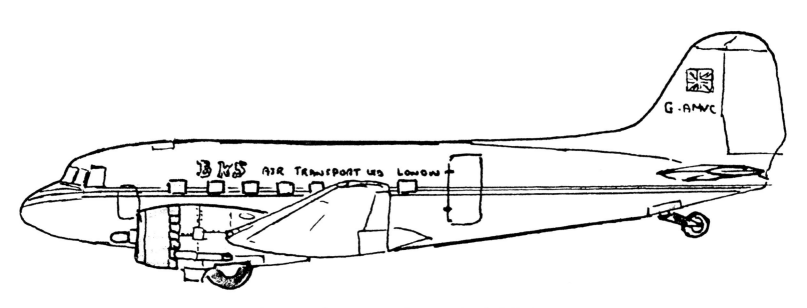

A common sight in post war civil aviation – Douglas DC3 (C47).

problem at the airport, and new parking aprons were added. On the passenger side an extension was built to the terminal capable of handling twice the number of passengers. By 1959, passengers using the terminal had risen to 44,740 while the aircraft movement had increased to 24,257. Air freight had increased as well to 320 metric tonnes which was a modest increase compared with movements and passengers.

Private light aircraft contributed a great deal to the movement figures, as by the late 'Fifties private flying had increased considerably. New aircraft companies' names appeared on the scene mostly from the United States, like Beech, Cessna and Piper. The British light aircraft had declined although there were still a number of Tiger Moths and Austers flying with a number of clubs. Leeds/Bradford was no exception. January 1959 saw the formation of Yorkshire Light Aircraft, whose purpose was to overhaul and maintain privately owned light aircraft that were becoming a common sight at the airport. At first Yorkshire Light Aircraft occupied two ex R.A.F. Bellman hangars, but when the hangars and surrounding buildings were demolished, the company moved to their purpose-built maintenance hangar on the southside of the airport.

With a generally renewed interest in private flying, 1959 saw the re-establishment of the Yorkshire Aeroplane Club who had been closely connected with the airport since its early days. It had declined through falling membership and high costs during the 'Fifties. In January 1959 permission was given by the Joint Airport Committee for the club to re-start its operations and they acquired new premises on the south-west side of the airport, just off the Harrogate Road.

During the 'Fifties a number of new small airlines appeared, like John Ruskins in Yorkshire Television's Airline series. One was North-South Airlines which during the summer of 1959 began a seasonal air service to Bournemouth and the Isle of Wight using either a 16 seater De Havilland Heron or Dakota, but due to lack of support, the service only lasted a short season — a few months. The following year because of financial problems the airline ceased operations altogether.

But for Leeds/Bradford, 1959 had been a remarkable year. Airlines had come and gone, but a number of new services were introduced. So within a decade most British and European destinations were within easy reach of Leeds/Bradford — Belfast, 1hr 25min — Bournemouth 1hr 30min — London 1hr 20min — Newquay 1hr 45min — Jersey 2hrs 45min — Brussels 2hrs 45min — Dublin 1hr 30min and Dusseldorf 3hrs. As all these flights were flown by piston airliners the outlook for the 'Sixties looked even more promising.

Over the next ten years the airport was to see further development, the introduction of new aircraft and the appearance of yet more new airlines.

Yeadon Aviation DH 89 Dragon Rapide parked outside the Municipal hangar.

Soon after the aerodrome returned to civilian use, Lancashire Aircraft Corporation began a summer service to the Isle of Man, as well as other charters from Yeadon. The photograph shows two of the company's newly acquired Rapides being prepared for flights.
Photograph courtesy of MAP.

A general view of the Municipal hangar taken in 1949.
Photograph courtesy of T & A.

The Fire section taken in 1950.

In 1955 Yeadon Aviation acquired some DH Rapides and began services from Yeadon. Here G.AIYE is being refuelled prior to a flight.
Photograph courtesy of MAP.

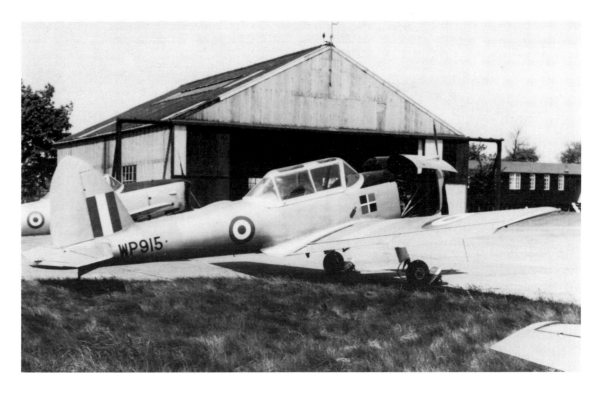

A DH Chipmunk trainer belonging to the Leeds University Squadron parked outside the airport's Robin Hangar.

Leeds University Squadron badge on the fuse. The squadron was formed at Yeadon in 1949 and remained at the aerodrome until eventually moving to RAF Finningley.

An aerial view of Yeadon 1957.
Photograph courtesy of C. H. Woods.

The Flying Club House with an Avro Anson parked in the background, taken mid 'Fifties.
Photograph courtesy of T & A.

A Percival Proctor of Airtaxi Ltd. was a frequent visitor to Yeadon during 1952.

Miles M2 Racer taken at an air display 1957.

During the 'Fifties, the Auster J/1 became a favourite aircraft with the flying club at Yeadon.

Silver City Airways Douglas C47 Dakota took over the Isle of Man summer schedule in 1957. The airline named G-AMJU – the City of Leeds. Photograph courtesy of E. Taylor.

A new airline – B.K.S. began services using the trusted Douglas C47 Dakota.

North-South Airlines Douglas C47 awaiting passengers.
Photograph courtesy of MAP.

A popular light twin-engined aircraft in the 'Fifties was the Miles Gemini, seen here parked outside the municipal hangar. Note the Spitfire parked in the distance.
Photograph courtesy of E. Taylor.

De Havilland DH82. Tiger Moths were a common sight throughout the 'Fifties.

Silver City Bristol Wayfarer landing on runway 10/28.
Photograph courtesy of MAP.

General view of private aircraft parked at Yeadon in 1958 with DH Tiger Moth G-AKXD in the foreground.
Photograph courtesy of E. Taylor.

THE 'SIXTIES

Civil aviation in the U.K. in the 'Sixties was most promising. Airlines were re-equipping with modern jet aircraft, and turbo props were replacing the older piston engine types on certain routes within the British Isles. B.O.A.C. had placed an order for the Vickers Super VC 10, which today has become a familiar sight at Leeds Bradford airport in the colours of the Royal Air Force on their trooping flights. B.E.A. had placed an order for the trijet D.H. 121 Trident to supplement its recently acquired 139-seater Vanguard, that was to replace the Viscount on its prestige routes. However L.B.A. did not benefit greatly from what was happening in the nationalised airlines, except perhaps later in the decade when British Airways Viscounts were found operating from the airport and a number of ex-B E.A. aircraft did appear in the livery of other airlines.

By now B.K.S. Air Transport had established itself in the country, especially in the north and it continued to expand its route network. Although it dropped its Leeds — London service some months earlier due to poor support, the airline felt that the 'Sixties was the right time to recommence the service on this prestige route; so in early 1960 one saw Douglas C47 in B.K.S. colours operating twice daily flights to the capital city. In April of the same year B.K.S. was joined by a new foreign airline to Leeds Bradford — Aer Lingus, the Irish national airline, on schedule flights to Dublin. Today various airlines often pool on certain routes, but in 1960 it was quite a unique achievement in the airline business. This partnership continued up until B.K.S. was absorbed by Northeast who dropped the route altogether, leaving Aer Lingus the sole operator. So the Irish airline's green-painted Dakotas were to become a common sight at L.B.A. for a number of years.

Passengers handled by the terminal in 1961 rose by over twenty-nine thousand air travellers on the previous year, while aircraft movements increased by nearly five thousand. Schedule flights continued to be the mainstay of the airport, but only increasing slightly. The most noticeable increase were the seasonal holiday flights especially to the Channel Islands, as well as some Continental destinations like Ostend and the Dutch bulb fields in the Spring.

While the airport and its staff were enjoying their deserved success, tragedy struck when in October 1961 a Leeds Bradford based B.K.S. Dakota G-AMVC crashed on the south-eastern side of Carlisle Airport killing its crew of four. The Dakota had been chartered by a group of farmers from the Carlisle area, but due to bad visibility the aircraft never reached its destination.

On 1st April 1962, and not an April's Fool trick, a new sound appeared over Leeds, when Aer Lingus introduced the first turbo prop airliner to the airport on their schedule flight from Dublin. The airline had only taken delivery of this new forty-seater Fokker F27 Friendship on 20th February. As the F27 was much faster than the conventional piston types like the Dakota, flying time to the Irish capital was reduced by nearly one half.

The F27 Friendship, built by the Dutch Aero Company, was powered by two Rolls Royce Dart turbo props with a speed of over 306 miles per hour and being pressurised provided its passengers with an extremely comfortable flight. No wonder the F27 became a success overnight. Today the Friendship has become a very familiar sight at Leeds Bradford, but now in the colours of Air U.K.

Although B.K.S. had seemed to be expanding in the early 'Sixties the company was in serious financial difficulties, so much so that by 1962 the receiver had been called in. After some considerable consideration it was decided that the company would not cease operations and was allowed to continue to trade, but was recommended to sell its assets including its fleet of Dakotas and to lease brand new Avro 748 and crews from Skyways. So at last B.K.S. had the modern turbo prop equipment to compete with the Fokker F27.

The Avro 748 was also powered by two Rolls Royce Dart R DA 514 giving 1740hp per engine. Over four hundred have been built and are in service with airlines all over the world. With speed in excess of 300 mph, B.K.S. had cut the flying time to London drastically and as with the F27, the aircraft were pressurised and flights became more tolerable.

These two turbo prop airliners dominated the market for years to come as the world airlines required modern equipment to replace their ageing Dakota fleets on feeder routes. Both aircraft proved very popular with both passengers and owners, who found them extremely economical to run compared with the piston types. By today's standard the Darts are regarded as very thirsty engines; therefore both types have been lengthened to accommodate more passengers and are powered by the more modern Pratt and Whitney turbo props engines to give us the British Aerospace A.T.P. and the Fokker F50. No doubt they will prove to be as popular and successful as their predecessors.

During the summer of 1962 Silver City Airways operated services to Jersey and the Isle of Man using their DC 3 or Bristol

Wayfarer, but sadly this was to be their last summer schedule, as before the end of the year the airline shares were taken over by Air Holdings Ltd., the parent company of British United Airlines of which the dynamic Freddie Laker had become the Managing Director. Although the take-over had occurred during the summer months, the name Silver City remained on the aircraft until the end of the year.

Another new turbo prop made an appearance at the airport in 1962, this being a Vickers Viscount of Starways of Liverpool, who operated a service between Leeds Bradford and Newquay during the summer months. The service was not really successful, and only lasted one short season. It is strange really that Starways chose to fly to Newquay; surely there must have been more popular destinations to choose from? Anyhow it gave the airport an opportunity to familiarise itself with the handling of the Viscount aircraft which was to be a regular visitor later.

The Vickers Viscount was the most successful of all British-built passenger aircraft and in the late 'Sixties, 'Seventies and 'Eighties became a common sight at most airports throughout the world. The last Viscount to operate from Leeds Bradford belonged to British Air Ferries in 1987, on charter flights to the Channel Islands. Nearly 450 Viscounts of all series were built and served faithfully with all the major airlines of the world. There are now only about fifty left in airline service throughout the world, with fifteen being owned by British Air Ferries. The first flight took place on 16th July 1948 when G AHRF the prototype took to the air on a faultless first flight powered by four Rolls Royce Darts. The 40-70 seater aircraft had a maximum speed of 330 mph, which gave it a considerable edge over most aircraft in service at the time. Its first debut at L.B.A. was on an unprofitable route, but it became a symbol of comfort and reliability, when it appeared first in the livery of Northeast, then British Airways and in later years with British Midland.

With the introduction of new heavier equipment and new routes, the Airport Committee felt there was a genuine need for further expansion at the airport. A new runway was urgently required, a new terminal to handle the increase in passengers and an up-grading of other amenities relevant to the smooth running of a modern airport. Leeds and Bradford Councils, as well as councillors of other towns and districts within West Yorkshire, were approached for financial support. As usual, there was a great deal of hostility towards the proposed plans, mostly from ratepayers living in the vicinity of the airport. So much so that at one point Wakefield Chambers of Commerce suggested that any further development at the airport would be a waste of money and would be better spent on developing a completely new site

such as Elvington which had already a superb 9,800ft runway and was only used as a relief landing ground for Church Fenton. However, after some heated and useful discussion, the go-ahead was finally given for the development at Leeds Bradford Airport.

It was not until October 1963 that work really started on the new 5,400ft runway 15/33 and it was completed in April 1965 ready for the usual summer seasonal flights. The new terminal took a little longer as work did not begin until December and then it only became priority as a result of the fire on 8th May 1965 when all the main passenger accommodation was totally destroyed. Temporary premises were constructed in part of the old Avro flight shed, but were inadequate. Surprisingly while all the construction work took place, the running of the airport was not affected.

During 1964 the Isle of Man service was taken over by British United (Manx) Airways using their trusted Dakotas although their Dart powered Handley Page Heralds were used quite frequently. British United had kept the Isle of Man — Leeds licence, when the company took over Silver City some years previously.

It was not only the airlines that were contributing to the success of the airport, private flying had increased considerably during the last few years. So much so that in July 1965 Yorkshire Light Aircraft decided to expand their business. New premises were acquired and a new maintenance hangar was built on the southside of the aiport. In later years this expanding business was to become the main distributor for Rolls Royce/Continental light engines and was to be the appointed agent and service centre for the American Piper light aircraft.

1964 was the year another local aircraft business was formed at Leeds Bradford Airport. This was the Northair Aviation Group formed by E. Crabtree and it traded as Northern Air Taxi until adopting its present title. Northair was another of Yorkshire's success stories, building a new headquarters and a maintenance hangar as well as their own passenger terminal for their taxi service which was their main activity. Later the firm became the north's main agents for the famous Cessna Aircraft Company which is a household name in the light aircraft business.

On St. George's Day 1966 the airport had a very unusual visitor in the shape of a U.S.N. Lockheed C121J Constellation. The aircraft based in Iceland was on a return journey from Spain where it had been involved in the search for the B52 and its nuclear weapons that crashed just off the Spanish Coast.

On 20th July 1967 the new control tower became operational. At last the airport had an up-to-date tower equipped with the latest communication and navigational aids. The same year the

East Midland based airline, British Midland, which just recently changed its name from Derby Airways began an East Midland to Leeds schedule service using either a Viscount or a Herald. This was to be the beginning of close links between the airline and the airport.

In 1967 B.K.S. introduced a new all-freight weekday service between Leeds Bradford and Belfast, textiles being the main cargo. The aircraft used was a converted Avro 748 with its seats removed. Soon afterwards Aer Lingus started a system of palletisation using a specially converted Viscount in a passenger cum/freighter role, able to carry 52 passengers plus 2 pallets of freight on their Dublin service. As a result, both airlines contributed a great deal to the total freight handled by the airport during the next few years.

It was not only freight that had a boom time during 1967. Passengers handled by the terminal rose to a staggering 298,060, while aircraft movement rose to a peak of 42,788.

Finally Leeds Bradford was blessed with the new passenger terminal which it urgently needed. The magnificent building costing £530,000 and capable of handling over 400 passengers per hour was officially opened by the Rt. Hon. Earl of Scarborough —the Lord Lieutenant of the West Riding on 3rd May 1968. Also in attendance were Ald. J. H. Behrens, Chairman of the Airport Committee, Mr. G. P. Sellers of course, the Airport Director, together with dignitaries from all over West Yorkshire. The opening was given extended press coverage, not only by the local papers, *Yorkshire Post* and the *Telegraph* and *Argus*, but by some of the national press including *The Guardian*.

The passenger terminal was an extremely modern complex and was regarded by many as one of the most modern air terminals in the U.K. The airport restaurant became renowned by both passengers and visitors alike, with first-class food and a superb view overlooking the apron. On the rear wall was a mural creation in ceramic and stone which extended for some eight feet along the rear of the viewing deck, nine feet high. It was created by Philippa Threlfall who was well-known for such work. On the outside next to the terminal was a viewing deck for plane-spotters with its own refreshment kiosk. This was ideal, but I am afraid today it is no longer there.

On the wall separating the restaurant and the viewing deck a memorial plaque was erected to commemorate No.609 Squadron which had such a close connection with Yeadon for many years.

With the increase in air travellers and the prospect of the introduction of jet aircraft, a special meeting of the Airport Joint Committee was held on 24th May 1968 when it was agreed to recommend an extension of the main NW/SE runway to a length of about 7,300ft.

For the rest of the 'Sixties the regular schedule flights continued to various destinations in the U.K. ranging from Belfast and Dublin to East Midlands and London, while the continental destinations included Amsterdam, Dusseldorf, Ostend and Paris. The summer seasonal flights provided the people of West Yorkshire with destinations to the Channel Islands, Isle of Man and for the first time I.T. flights to Spain —Barcelona, Gerona and Palma. At last Leeds Bradford was in the International league.

Regular airlines using the airport towards the end of the 'Sixties were the usual names like Aer Lingus, B.K.S., B.M.A. and B.U. (CI) A. on the schedule services, while names like Air Ferry, Channel Airways, Invicta, Air Links and Martin Air Charter provided the I.T. flights.

Towards the end of the decade B.K.S. disappeared from Leeds, its London service being taken over by Northeast, a name that would be quite familiar at Leeds for some years to come. B.K.S., although dogged by financial trouble earlier, managed to continue to provide air service in the North of England. Reflecting its assocation with the north eastern corner of Britain, the airline was renamed Northeast. So from 1st November 1979 the new yellow white and grey livery of the airline became a common sight, with its reliable and comfortable Viscount on London and Newcastle flights.

It was not long before Northeast had been taken over by the British Air Service, which had been set up by British European Airways to look after other domestic airlines. The Welsh, Cambrian Airways, had become a wholly owned subsidiary of B.A.S. a year earlier, but both airlines were allowed to keep their separate identities and livery for the time being at least.

Another airline changed its name in 1968. The Manx and Channel Island division of British United became British United (Islands) Airways, but the name did not appear at L.B.A. until the following year.

Reflecting on the 'Sixties, it turned out to be quite an eventful decade. The airport had a new runway added, and a new control tower as well as a brand new passenger terminal. Passengers handled by the airport had gone up from 77,063 in 1960 to a staggering 297,037 in 1969, aircraft movement from 22,025 to 38,493 and freight had increased from a mere 546 metric tonnes to 2,137 tonnes in 1969. At last Leeds Bradford airport had an extremely rosy future, thanks to Mr. Sellers and his loyal, enthusiastic staff.

The 'Sixties also turned out to be the beginning of I.T. flights for L.B.A. The regular flight to the Isle of Man and the Channel Islands was always popular, especially when British United were advertising the 40min flights to the Isle of Man for a mere £3.12. one-way, in one of their turbo prop Heralds. But more distant flights to the Dutch bulb fields became quite popular during the Spring months. One had the opportunity to see a variety of different airlines and aircraft using the airport including the Dutch company Martinair with its Dakotas and, a very rare aircraft, a Rolls Royce Dart powered Convair 440. There were also Sterling Airways DC4 and DC6, and Invicta Airways DC4 and Viscount flights to Ostend. There were also some airlines that only appeared for a short season like Treffield Aviation, whose Viscount made regular visits to the airport.

Jet aircraft did make a brief appearance towards the end of the decade, but due to the length of the runway could not take off fully loaded.

Even in the early 'Sixties, Tiger Moths and Austers were commonly used by a number of flying clubs and individuals.
Photograph courtesy of MAP.

Fly British United to the **Isle of Man** from Leeds/Bradford for as little as **£3.12.**

(lowest single Tourist Class fare)

Just **45 easy minutes** and you're abroad in the Isle of Man.

Ask your Travel Agent for

BUA ◄
BRITISH UNITED AIRWAYS
Bardon Chambers, Infirmary Street, Leeds
Tel: (0532) 39124/6.

People who know go **BUA**

A 1969 advert for British United Airways.

In the early 'Sixties Derby Airways (forerunner to British Midland) Douglas C47 Dakota made its debut at Yeadon, when the airline began a daily schedule service between Derby, Leeds and Glasgow. Photograph courtesy of BMA.

Aer Lingus Douglas Dakota began a Leeds-Dublin schedule flight in the early 'Sixties and has continued to keep its close ties with the airport until today.
Photograph courtesy of Aer Lingus.

General view of the apron during the spring of 1963 with BEA Viscount, BKS Douglas C46, British United Heralds and Air Links Argonaut that were used on charter flights to Lourdes.
Photograph courtesy of *Yorkshire Post.*

When Aer Lingus began using Fokker F27 on their Dublin flights, BKS introduced the new Avro 748 turbo prop airliners to compete.

Dan Air Airspeed Ambassadors were used on the early IT charter flights from the airport especially to the Dutch bulb fields and Paris.
Photograph courtesy of Dan Air.

Vickers Viscounts belonging to Starways were used on schedule flights to Newquay during a brief period in 1962.
Photograph courtesy of MAP.

An unusual visitor to the airport in 1966 was a U.S.N. Lockheed C121J Constellation when it made a brief refuelling stop.

British United Airways H.P. Herald awaiting to take off on a flight to Jersey.

Another unusual sight – three Sabena Douglas DC 6B parked at the airport. The aircraft brought Belgian supporters to Elland Road for a match against Leeds United.
Photograph courtesy of A. Hill.

Invicta Air Cargo, Douglas DC4 were used mostly on cargo flights to the Channel Islands and Holland. Photograph courtesy of C. Walker.

In the second half of the 'Sixties BKS changed their name to Northeast Airlines. Photograph shows one of the airline's Vicker Viscounts on the London service.

Northern Air Taxi or Northair as it was known brought a lot of business to the airport.
Here a Beagle B206 is ready for its next passengers.
Photograph courtesy of Northair.

THE 'SEVENTIES

By the 1970's, the majority of airlines were re-equipping with modern jet airliners like the Boeing 737 and the B.A.C.1-11. Many regional airports were found unsuitable for jet operations, and major rebuilding, resurfacing and extensions were taking place all over the British Isles.

The runways of Leeds Bradford were a predicament. A new runway had been completed only seven years earlier, but by the early 'Seventies it was far from being of a sufficient length to cope with the new breed of heavier jet equipment that required newer safety margins. As the result of a meeting of the Airport Joint Committee held in May 1968, plans were put forward for extending runway 14/32 to meet these new standards, but as usual the airport was faced with considerable objections to the plans from some of the local residents especially those living on the airport approaches. At one stage salesmen at a newly built housing estate assured potential buyers that the airport would eventually close. It was not only the local residents that objected to the proposed plans, even some of the councillors were against investing more ratepayers' money in the airport.

So the proposed extension, that was vital to the future of L.B.A. faced a bitter resistance from several quarters, and after numerous heated debates and a Public Enquiry, the proposal was sent to the Department of Transport who had the final say. In October 1970 Mr. Peter Walker, who was then the Minister responsible, turned down the application, therefore depriving the airport of a promising future. As one saw in later years, not only the airport and air transport suffered, but various light industries in the Leeds Bradford area. The anti-airport supporters had won the first round.

It took another ten years before L.B.A. eventually got its 2,000ft extension, and then after another bitter fight with the same objectors, but the damage had been done. Other regional airports in the south and the north-east were developed and extended and attracted, not only new air services, but new industries and investment, which Leeds and Bradford could have done with.

Meanwhile the airport kept on functioning. The regular airlines still flew from Leeds Bradford and although there was disappointment over Peter Walker's decision, the Airport Committee never gave up, but carried on promoting the airport and the area to the country.

By 1970 Aer Lingus was the sole operator on the Dublin route, and as the airline had been the first to introduce turbo prop to the airport years earlier it too became the first to use jet equipment. Its B.A.C.1-11 or Boeing 737-200 were used on the weekday flights to the Irish capital, but due to the length of the runway the aircraft had to be operated at a lower operating weight. At the outset the load factor was quite high, but as the novelty wore off Aer Lingus found it increasingly difficult to fill all the seats on an aircraft the size of a Boeing 737, and the smaller One Eleven was mostly used.

The name B.K.S. had completely disappeared by the early 'Seventies. All the 748's had been returned to Skyways and the Northeast Viscount became the most common sight at the airport. Although Northeast was based at Newcastle it regarded Leeds Bradford as its second home.

In 1972 British Midland, who had become a regular user of the airport since its days when it traded as Derby Airways, withdrew its East Midlands-Leeds-Glasgow service, depriving the area of an air link to Scotland and the Midlands. The Scottish route soon attracted another operator, this being Dan Air, who had occasionally operated I.T. flights for various travel firms in previous years and who had been waiting for an opportunity to include Leeds Bradford in its route network. Therefore on 4th April 1972 a Hawker Siddeley (Avro) 748 G-ARAY operated a proving flight on the new route Luton-Leeds-Glasgow and was officially inaugurated a week later on the 11th April. The 748 operated by Dan Air had been previously used by B.K.S., as Skyways International with its fleet had been acquired by Dan Air during 1972. Leeds Bradford benefited a great deal by the arrival of this new airline, as it brought with it ground handling and engineering facilities which have remained at the airport until today.

On 10th April 1972 British Airways' Board was formed to centralise all national and international services operated by B.E.A. and B.O.A.C. As a result all British Air Service interests came under the control of British Airways Regional Division, and Cambrian and Northeast disappeared altogether with the routes being taken over by B.E.A. Northeast was more fortunate than its Welsh counterpart Cambrian Airways. The northern airline kept its identity rather longer, but it too disappeared and B.E.A. took over the London route using Viscounts.

With the disappearance of one airline, another new name appeared on the scene. It was in 1974 that the Norwich based Air Anglia made its debut at Leeds Bradford Airport, when on 6th May the airline began a scheduled weekday service from Norwich to Edinburgh and Aberdeen via Leeds. The aircraft used on this inaugural flight was a Fokker F27 Friendship — G-BAUR which was to become a regular visitor to the airport for years to come. As a matter of fact the aircraft is still used today by Air U.K. on its domestic and international flights.

An increase in the cost of aviation fuel in the latter half of 1973 and early 1974 did not prevent Leeds Bradford having another extremely good year. A total of 44,435 aircraft movements took place, while the terminal handled 283,570 passengers. It was not perhaps as good a year as 1967, but everything looked encouraging; new airlines were waiting in the wings so to speak to begin brand new services to destinations not covered.

There had not been any air links to the south-west corner of Britain since the early 'Sixties when Starways of Liverpool operated a seasonal service to Newquay. In 1975 a new airline based at Bristol — Severn Airways whose fleet included two aircraft, a Piper Navajo G-BBDU and a De Havilland Dove G-APSK, acquired a licence to operate a service between Leeds/Bradford and Bristol. The first proving flight on the 18th March turned out to be a grand public occasion. The Lord Mayor of Bristol, Councillor A. G. Pegler, flew to Leeds where he was met by the Lord Mayors of both Leeds and Bradford, and after a civic reception made the return flight to Bristol. The Dove, piloted by Pilot Officer S. Lefont, took 75 mins but the return journey took just over an hour. The actual daily service commenced a week later with a return fare of £23.50, but by the end of the month had increased to £28. As the airline was so pleased with the response, it put forward plans to extend the service to Cork from Bristol, with the 5th May as a target date; but this never materialised. Even the service to Leeds was withdrawn in July 1975, not because of poor support, but because of financial problems within the airline. Soon afterwards Severn Airways ceased operations altogether, a very sad ending to a brave attempt.

1975 turned out to be an average year for the airport. Aircraft movement had increased mostly due to private flying, while passengers using the airport had dropped by nearly five and a half thousand. Some new services were introduced, but they did not counteract the routes that were dropped. Seasonal flights still contributed most to the overhaul total. But sadly freight was very disappointing. Since the early 'Seventies, it had been on the downward trend and by 1975 it was down to a mere 621 metric tonnes.

Since the withdrawal of the Bristol service the previous year Dan Air had been assessing the route to the South West and to Cardiff in particular. So, in 1976 the airline recommenced the service as a daily weekday flight, and for the first time linking Leeds with the Welsh capital.

This historical first flight took place on 6th January 1976 with a Leeds to Cardiff and Leeds to Bristol service, but the return flight to L.B.A. extended on to Glasgow. The aircraft used on these first flights were two Hawker Siddeley 748 G-ARAY and G-BEBA.

Regular schedule services to the Channel Islands had lapsed since the disappearance of Silver City Airways. The summer seasonal flights had more or less continued but the all year round service did not exist. Therefore Air Anglia decided the time was right to introduce a regular service to Jersey, the first being on 27th October 1976 using the F27 G-BAUR. Also during 1976 Air Anglia which by now had become one of the major users of the airport began a schedule service to Amsterdam. The aircraft used on this inaugural flight was a F27 G-BCDO.

While the majority of regional airports in the U.K. were benefiting from holiday charter flights to the Mediterranean resorts, Leeds Bradford was not so fortunate. Up to then, only the occasional I.T. flights had taken place and were mostly to holiday destinations in Northern Europe like Ostend or the Dutch bulb fields. One of the reasons was that airlines were in the process of replacing the older piston engine airliners with the fast and modern jet equipment, and were reluctant to use the aircraft on such flights from Leeds Bradford Airport.

In November 1976 Britannia Airways Boeing 737-200 series, on behalf of Thomson Holidays took off for Palma on their first ever I.T. flight from the airport. This became the beginning of regular holiday flights by both Thomson and Britannia, and by today thousands upon thousands of holiday-makers have flown with the two companies from L.B.A. to various holiday destinations, not only during the summer season but throughout the year.

Thomson must have made quite an impression, as soon afterwards other tour operators became increasingly interested in operating out of the airport.

British Island Airways made a brief appearance during the summer of 1976, when the airline began a schedule service to Bournemouth with connections to the Channel Islands, but due to poor support the service only lasted for one season.

By 1978 Air Anglia had decided to pull out of the Channel Island service as their aircraft were required elsewhere on more profitable and busier routes. Once again Dan Air saw an opportunity to expand their network routes especially in the north of England, and on 15th April 1978 they began to operate a schedule service from Leeds to Jersey. The aircraft used on this first flight was a 44 seater Hawker Siddeley 748 registration number G-BEKG.

Another international route was added to Leeds Bradford's

growing list of destinations in 1978, when on 2nd May Air Anglia Fokker F27 G-BDVT made the first flight to Paris. Air U.K. has kept this prestigious route ever since and by today it has become one of the most important destinations with the airline.

Towards the end of 1974 British Airways (B.E.A.) had ceased to operate the Leeds-London Heathrow service, and British Midland acquired the licence for the route, which they still hold today. After an absence of some years, this East Midland based airline became a familiar sight at the airport with its Viscounts and F27 which were used on the newly acquired route.

With the appearance of this strange airline at Leeds Bradford, Air Anglia decided to introduce some competition, and on 3rd November 1979 a Leeds-London Gatwick schedule service was begun using an F27. Within a month due to poor support the airline decided a smaller capacity aircraft was required on the route, and on 17th December a newly purchased EMB 110 Bandeirante (G-BGYS) was substituted. This 19 seater Brazilian built airliner was found quite suitable for this particular low density route, but response was still poor as the majority of air travellers still regarded Heathrow as London's airport and were not prepared to fly so far south.

By the end of the 'Seventies, there was a large change taking place in the airline business, just like years earlier when British United took over a number of smaller airlines. This time it was the aviation interests of the British and Commonwealth Shipping Group being combined into one organisation. British Island Airways was combined with Air Anglia, Air Wales and Air West to form Air U.K. giving the new company a better opportunity to compete with other airlines both in the domestic and international market. So the familiar name of Air Anglia was to disappear from the airport forever, although both names did appear for a while during the transition period.

Another decade had gone in the life of the airport, during which time several new airlines had appeared adding new destinations to L.B.A. departure boards. Also a few well-known names had completely disappeared, swallowed up by the multi-giants. The 'Seventies would be mostly remembered for the introduction of the jet airliner which had transformed air travelling overnight, and from now on holiday charter flights were going to form the major revenue for the airport.

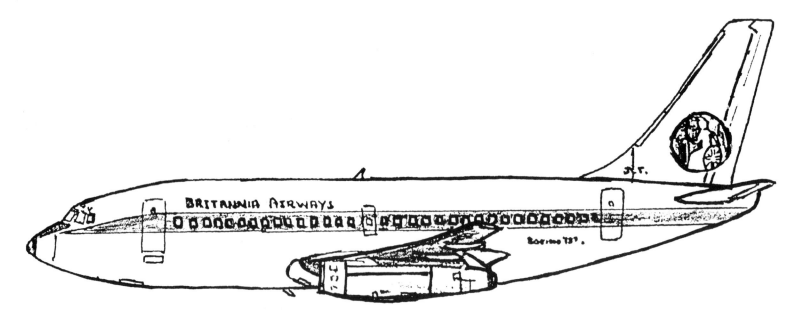

Britannia Airways Boeing 737-200.

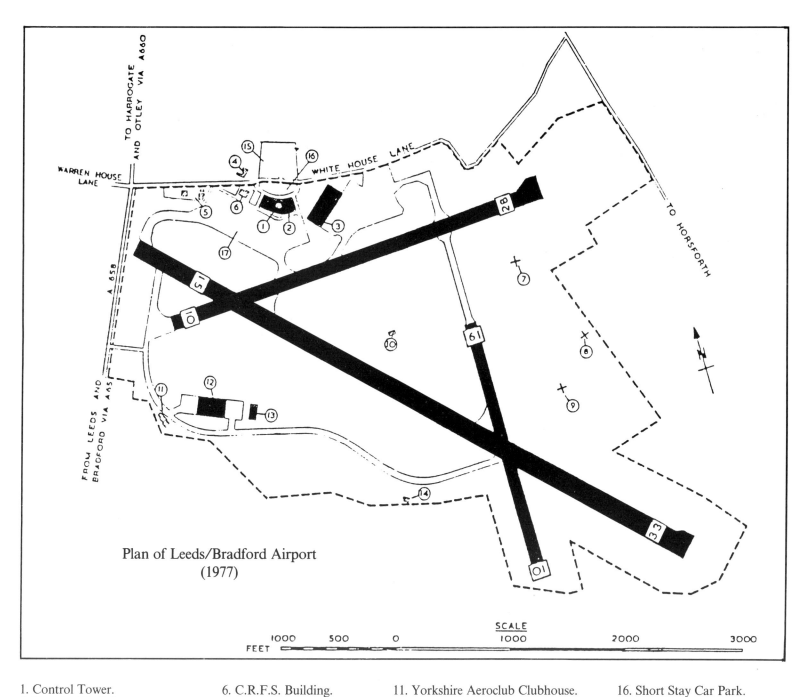

Plan of Leeds/Bradford Airport
(1977)

SCALE

| 1000 | 500 | 0 | | 1000 | 2000 | 3000 |

FEET

1. Control Tower.
2. Terminal Building.
3. Freight Shed.
4. Boiler House.
5. S.M./B.P. Refuelling Depot.
6. C.R.F.S. Building.
7. C.R.D.F.
8. Identification Beacon.
9. Anemometer.
10. Radar Scanner.
11. Yorkshire Aeroclub Clubhouse.
12. Yorkshire Light Aircraft Hangar.
13. Northair Aviation Hangar.
14. V.H.F. Receiving Station.
15. Long Stay Car Park.
16. Short Stay Car Park.
17. Apron.

Dan Air Hawker Siddeley 748
G-ARAY was used on the airline's
proving flight between Luton-Leeds-
Glasgow on 4th April 1972.
Photograph courtesy of Dan Air.

Air Anglia Fokker F27
on a wintery morning.
Photograph courtesy of Air U.K.

*Pan Adria Convair 440 Metropolitan, used
on the first ever I.T. flight to Yugoslavia.*
Photograph courtesy of C. Walker.

*Aer Lingus was the first to introduce jet
equipment to Leeds Bradford Airport in
the shape of a B.A.C. One eleven.*
Photograph courtesy of Aer Lingus.

Novelist Brian Lecumber in his Stamp SV4 during a publicity visit to the airport. Photograph courtesy of C. Walker.

Not long after the introduction of the One Eleven, Aer Lingus used its newly acquired Boeing 737-200 on the Dublin flight giving the airport a foretaste of the type of aircraft that was to dominate airline business in years to come. Photograph courtesy of Aer Lingus.

Blackburn B2 belonging to Lt. Cdr. Whithead prior to his long-distance flight to New York.
Photograph courtesy of C. Walker.

Another view of the Blackburn B2 with two British Air Service Viscounts in the background.
Photograph courtesy of C. Walker.

Severn Airways De Havilland Dove began a schedule service to Bristol and Cardiff in May 1975.
Photograph courtesy of R. Williams.

In the mid-Seventies British Midland acquired the London-Heathrow licence and used their Vickers Viscount on the service.
Photograph courtesy of BMA.

Aerial view of Leeds Bradford Airport 1977. Note the two Viscounts in front of the terminal with the old black painted flight shed to its right. In the foreground are the Yorkshire Light Aircraft and Northair hangars. In the left-hand corner is the wartime Avro shadow Factory.
Photograph courtesy of C. H. Wood.

General view of the apron taken 2nd November 1979. While Manchester Airport was fog bound a number of flights were diverted to Leeds Bradford Airport, a sight that not only would please every aircraft spotter but any Airport Director as well.
Photograph courtesy of T & A.

Northair Cessna 310G parked in front of the terminal. Private flying still contributed a great deal of revenue to the airport in the 'Seventies.
Photograph courtesy of Northair.

British Midland used its Fokker F27 on the London flights especially at the weekends.
Photograph courtesy of BMA.

On the 17th December 1979 Air Anglia introduced its EMB 110 Bandeirante on the Leeds Bradford to London Gatwick service. Within a month their aircraft appeared in the new livery.
Photograph courtesy of Air U.K.

To advertise the T.V. programme "Double Your Money", Hughie Green and his delightful hostesses line-up for a publicity photo aboard a B.E.A. Viscount at Leeds Bradford Airport.
Photograph courtesy of C. Walker.

THE 'EIGHTIES

The 'Eighties began as a recurrence of the 'Seventies. An extended runway and a new larger terminal were urgently required if Leeds Bradford Airport was to compete profitably with other regional airports and cope with the predicted increase in traffic. There was still a considerable amount of hostility from some of the local residents who by now had gathered quite a support.

The Airport Committee had realised that to make L.B.A. successful and to attract new business the proposed expansion had to go ahead. Already schedule flights to various destinations in the U.K. as well as abroad had nearly doubled in the last ten years.

Ever since the introduction of the first direct holiday flight to the Mediterranean by Britannia Airways for Thomson Holidays in 1976, the Committee foresaw that such holiday charter flights were going to be one of the main sources of revenue for the airport in future years. By the early 'Eighties other major tour operators were becoming increasingly interested in operating from Leeds Bradford and it was not too long before the Airport appeared in holiday brochures of Intasun, Arrowsmith, Horizon and Yugotours.

The 'Eighties turned out to be a memorable decade for the airport. L.B.A. eventually got its runway extension, new terminal, even extended operating hours. New airlines and new aircraft opened up new routes, traffic increased on existing domestic and continental routes and even more cargo was handled, although still considerably less than other regional airports of the same size. But the 'Eighties will mostly be remembered for the new aircraft that made their debut at the airport including the Boeing 747 Jumbo Jet, the Tristar, Boeing 757, the European Airbus and of course the pride of all modern jet airlines, the Concorde.

It was in the early 'eighties that the airport got its new director when in the Spring of 1982 Mr. Gordon Dennison took over from Mr. G. P. Sellers who had to retire due to ill health after completing twenty years as Airport Director.

Lancashire born, Gordon Dennison had his background training for civil aviation in the Royal Air Force which helped him a great deal to achieve his new position. During his national Service in the R.A.F., he trained to be an engineer, but had always an ambition to become aircrew. His dream came true in 1952 when he began his flight training and eventually passed out as an Air Navigator, serving mostly in English Electric Canberra bombers both at home and abroad.

After completing twelve years in the R.A.F., he felt it was time to seek other avenues, especially in Civil Aviation, and as Air Traffic Control had always fascinated him, he decided to join these highly trained operators. In front of him were months of training with the Civil Aviation Authority, and being an R.A.F. trained navigator helped him a great deal with the very arduous course which he passed with ease.

During the next three years Gordon Dennison served as A.T.C. at a number of airports throughout Britain ranging from Birmingham, Belfast, Bournemouth, Gatwick and Liverpool. He eventually joined the Controllers at Leeds Bradford Airport in 1967 as a Junior Air Traffic Controller. Within a few years he became the Operation Officer, and during the next ten years or so he became involved in the general day-to-day running of the airport, including the introduction of jet equipment at L.B.A. as well as the introduction of new airlines and new routes which had begun during the 'Seventies.

In 1981 Gordon Dennison had an opportunity to fill the Director's post on a temporary basis and when the post finally became vacant a year later he was the obvious choice.

As Airport Director, he was fortunate to witness a great change at the airport, most of which can be credited to his sheer determination.

By 1980 there had been a steady increase in traffic. Over two million passengers had already used the terminal since it was opened in 1968 and the prospects looked even better for the 'Eighties. It was obvious that the terminal was not going to cope with the increase in passenger traffic, the result being that new businesses and airlines would choose alternative airports, depriving the area of needed investment. This was one of the points put forward to the Minister of Transport who had the final say, but it took further debate as well as a public hearing before the Minister gave the go-ahead in January 1981.

Once the green light was given and not to waste precious time tenders were immediately put out to various contractors.

This massive £25 million investment was to secure the future of the airport and bring it into line with other major airports in the United Kingdom. Half the amount was obtained from Common Market grants, while the rest was met by the ratepayers of West Yorkshire. At the time this was the biggest investment ever to be undertaken in the area.

The breakdown of this huge investment was as follows:- £8.5 million was to be spent on the runway extension, which meant a tunnel had to be built to take the A658 access road. This contributed to most of the total cost. As this was a major road linking Leeds with Harrogate and Otley, it had to be a four lane carriage-way. £4 million was spent on the freight area, a complete new building being required to replace the old wartime hangar which had been used. New navigation lights had been long overdue as well as new apron lights. The above amount also covered the cost of extending the parking apron.

Another £4 million was spent on a new updated radar which the airport had to have to cope with the proposed increase in traffic. New firetenders, snowploughs and other airport vehicles were included in the shopping list, as well as a new car park.

To handle the increase in passengers that was inevitable, a new terminal had to be constructed, while the existing one was to be modified and modernised. The total bill for all this came to around £5 million.

Finally £3.5 million was spent on the cost of acquiring new land, profesional fees etc. and a large proportion was allocated for anti-noise measures to try and please some of the local residents, especially those living in the close vicinity of the airport and on the runway approaches.

Therefore in 1982 work began on extending runway 14/32 by 2,000ft bringing it up to 7,380ft. Even after the bulldozers had moved in there was still an outcry and protests from the anti-airport lobby. Work also started on extending and modernising the terminal, but while all the construction work was taking place, the airport continued to function with its day-to-day running. Not once did any flight have to be cancelled because of the work.

One personality that stood out more than most people during the extension programme was Roy Minear, a graduate in Civil Engineering of Birmingham University, who became involved in co-ordinating detailed design work for the runway, apron and terminal building extensions. When construction finally began he was appointed the Project Manager — whose task was to be a day-to-day link between the Airport Director and the Resident Engineer, Architect and contractors on site.

Roy Minear's assocation with Leeds Bradford goes back to April 1966 when he was appointed an Assistant Resident Engineer for the construction of the new apron, the terminal area and rebuilding of the subsidiary runways 10/28 and 01/19. A year later he was made Resident Engineer for the completion of the extension and redevelopment, and the installation of airfield lighting.

For the next six years he continued his involvement with the airport as a Project Engineer with Leeds City Engineers Department — Transportation Unit, by providing technical support to the Airport Director in various forms. Therefore when the 'Eighties extension programme came along, Roy Minear was the obvious choice due to his previous experience.

In February 1985 he was awarded for his earlier achievement by being appointed Assistant Airport Director (Administration and Finance). His duties included the supervision of all financial matters, apron handling, security and terminal operations.

It was partly due to Roy Minear's work at the airport that when the extension scheme was completed in November 1984, it won the Institution of Civil Engineers' Award for excellence in concept, design and execution of work which today can be seen in the entrance to the first floor restaurant.

In July 1987 Roy Minear left Leeds Bradford Airport to become Managing Director of Humberside Airport, where he remained until July 1989. Today he is the Managing Director of Blackpool Airport, which at the time of writing is in the middle of an extension programme.

Total passengers handled during 1981 were only 351,000 a rather disappointing total considering Leeds Bradford had such a large catchment area, compared with Newcastle Airport which handled well over twice the number during the same period, mostly due to an increase in I.T. holiday charters.

During the early 'Eighties there was a fairly reasonable air service between Leeds Bradford and London, with British Midland serving Heathrow and Air U.K. Stansted. Both these airports however, were on the north and western edge of the capital city, and it was felt that a connection to the south and south-east corner of England was urgently required. Therefore in 1982 a new airline came on the scene. Genair began a twice daily service to London Gatwick using a 33 seater Short 3.30. Traffic on the route was quite encouraging with a high load factor on most flights. So Genair became a regular user of the airport until 1984 when due to financial problems, not necesarily because of the Leeds service, it ceased operations.

It was not only Genair who had been pleased with the London service. According to British Midland, one service that gave cause for particular satisfaction was Heathrow to Leeds Bradford. This service recorded a quite substantial 27 per cent growth in passenger traffic and announced that it planned to introduce a DC 9 instead of Viscounts on the route as soon as the runway extension was completed. The news delighted the airport authorities, as it would establish the airport's first regular true jet schedule service.

On the private flying side, May 1982 saw the take-over of the air taxi operator M.H.G. International by Mountleigh Group who had become the major shareholder in the company. Its sole

Cessna 414 Chancellor became the property of its new owners Mountleigh Air Services.

In 1983 the West Yorkshire based Brown Group of Companies formed a new company, Brown Air based at the airport. At first it started operations as an air taxi service, but on 1st October 1984 it began a Leeds-Oslo schedule service using a Cessna 441 Conquest (G-MOXY). Flights to Frankfurt with stops at Humberside soon followed.

With the collapse of Genair in June 1984 another northern commuter airline Air Ecosse saw the potential of the London Gatwick service and within a matter of months took over the route. For the next few years Air Ecosse Short 3.30 and Bandeirantes served Leeds Bradford with London Gatwick as well as Humberside, until 1986 when the airline withdrew from the scheduled scene.

Also in 1984 two feeder air services were formed in the U.K., Connectair and Metropolitan Airways, the idea being for these small commuter airlines to connect regional airports with the main international airports like London, Manchester and Birmingham.

Metropolitan Airways, with the assistance of Dan Air, began feeder services connecting Glasgow, Leeds, Cardiff and Bristol. The first service was on 26th March 1984, Leeds to Glasgow and Leeds to Cardiff and Bristol using Short 3.30 (G-BGNA). Although Dan Air had been operating the route before, in recent years the service had lapsed and Metropolitan aircraft became a common sight at the airport. The service was quite successful, but sadly like Genair the airline ceased operations in August 1985. It is difficult to understand the reason, but it seemed that Dan Air was not prepared to back the airline indefinitely, whereas Connectair flourished and was eventually sold by British Caledonian Airways.

The road tunnel built to take the A658 road underneath the extended runway 14/32 was officially opened on 1st March 1984 by Councillor T. E. Hall, who was the Chairman of the Airport Committee, but it would be another year before the runway would be ready for operation. The first aircraft to officially use the new extended runway was British Airways Boeing 747 which became the first Jumbo jet to use the airport.

Up to 1984 Aer Lingus had been using either Fokker F27, Viscounts or, on occasions, One-Elevens on the Dublin service, but it too found that traffic did not justify such large capacity aircraft. By now Aer Lingus Commuter had been formed to operate services to U.K. regional airports from points in Eire. Therefore on 30th March 1984 the airline introduced the new Short 3.60 (EL-BEL "St. Avite") to Leeds Bradford Airport and

this together with the airline's other 3.60's have been frequent visitors to the airport ever since.

Only a handful of I.T. flights to Mediterranean destinations had been available until the runway extension, using mostly Boeing 737 or B.A.C. One-Elevens, and then operating on lower take off weights. Now there was an opportunity to persuade tour operators to operate more flights from Leeds Bradford, as during a survey conducted some years before the majority of holiday-makers living this side of the Pennines said they would prefer to fly from Leeds.

1985 witnessed a sharp increase in I.T. holiday charters from the airport and it seemed a little persuasion had worked.

Up till then Britannia Airways had only been using Boeing 737's on all their holiday flights from Leeds Bradford, but on 2nd May 1985 their new Boeing 767 G-BLKW, which had only been delivered in March, made its first appearance at the airport. For an unexplained reason, however, Britannia's B767 was not to appear at the airport again, for some years.

In the same year British Airways introduced the Lockheed Tristar to Leeds Bradford, the first flight being on 6th May 1985 when G-BBAJ made its appearance. On 27th May, B. A. Tristar G-BBAI was involved in a mishap. The aircraft was on an inbound flight from Palma with 416 passengers aboard, most of whom lived in the West Yorkshire area. During landing on a rather wet and slippery runway, in blustery rainy conditions it ran off the end of runway 14/32. Within seconds the airport emergency service as well as tenders from the airport's vicinity were on the scene and within a matter of minutes all the passengers had been evacuated from the aircraft. If it had not been for the magnificent handling of the aircraft by the pilot and its crew, as well as the quick reaction of the emergency service, the incident could have been a major disaster, even worse than the one experienced at Manchester Airport the year before when a British Airways 737 burst into flames after an aborted take-off due to engine failure. The result there was an appalling loss of life.

An inquiry took place to find the cause of the Tristar accident and after a lengthy period, it was more or less decided that the accident happened because of bad weather and a slippery runway due to the heavy rain.

At least there was better news for the airport during the summer months. The long-awaited phase one development of the Airport Terminal Building was finally completed and on Thursday 18th July 1985 it was officially opened by H.R.H. The Duchess of Kent.

Thankfully 1986 was not going to be remembered by a near-disasater, but as it turned out as a very eventful year. At last passengers handled rose to over half a million. Aircraft movements were less than the previous year, but larger capacity aircraft were being used, especially on I.T. holiday charter flights.

By now Air Ecosse had become fairly established at Leeds Bradford providing the area with air links to Teesside and Humberside using a Short 3.30. Brown Air having only started operations some years earlier, were eager to expand their services from Leeds Bradford, and in 1986 the C.A.A. awarded the airline licence to operate a Leeds to Glasgow service, which had been relinguished by Metropolitan Airways when it ceased operation. A leased Short 3.30 G-BEFO was used on the twice daily flight to Glasgow while the Cessna 441 Conquest G-MOXY were mostly used on the daily flight to Frankfurt and Oslo.

In January 1986 Brown Air had acquired a Gruman Gulfstream from Priester Aviation of Chicago, which was flown direct to Leeds Bradford by Brown Air crew. As the type was not certified in the U.K., it spent a long time receiving modifications to the satisfaction of the C.A.A. at Fields Aviation. This resulted in a very high cost by the time the aircraft entered service in September 1986. The Gulfstream registration G-BRWN was powered by two Rolls Royce Dart 529 giving the aircraft a reasonable speed of 348 mph, with ranges of up to 2,540 miles. The aircraft was to replace the 8-11 passenger Cessna 441 which was the most luxurious aircraft in the Cessna range, but the Gulfstream compared favourably and was ideal for Brown Air continental services.

Aer Lingus as usual operated the daily flights to Dublin using Short 3.60, occasionally using a higher capacity aircraft at weekends and holiday periods. But the bulk of schedule flights during 1986 were by Air U.K. Their F27 connecting Leeds Bradford with Aberdeen, Belfast, Edinburgh and Stansted in the British Isles, and Copenhagen, Amsterdam and Paris on the Continent. Weekend flights to Guernsey and Jersey were operated by Dan Air using their Hawker Siddeley 748. London's three airports were served well from West Yorkshire. British Midland operated five daily flights to Heathrow, by now using Douglas DC9 Srs.10, but they still used either a Viscount or F27 at the weekends. Gatwick was served by Air Ecosse using Short 3.30 on twice-daily flights and Air U.K. also operated a twice-daily flight to Stansted using F27.

Since the 'Thirties Yorkshire has always had an airlink with the Isle of Man, and during the early part of the 'Eighties Jersey European operated the Sunday service while Manx Airways operated the Saturday flights. Eventually Manx was to take over all the weekend flights.

No doubt, the year will be mostly remembered for two memorable events. Firstly, during the summer of 1986 one witnessed the beginning of the seasonal weekly service to Toronto, Canada by the Canadian Airline Wardair. Every Monday large crowds of spectators would wait in all weather to see the airline's Boeing 747 jumbo jet land and take off. As well as being the shortest 747 sector, between Leeds and Birmingham, Leeds Bradford was proud to become the smallest regional U.K. airport to operate a jumbo jet service.

Finally the goal of every regional airport took place in August 1986 when the first Concorde landed at Leeds Bradford. The honour went to Air France whose Concorde captained by Captain Raymond Machavoine made a perfect landing on runway 14/32. All advantage points around the airport were occupied by sightseers and every road leading to the airport was blocked. Even roads and areas over five miles away were congested with on-lookers; it seemed that the whole population of Yorkshire had come to see this wonderful event. Since that first prestigious visit, British Airways Concorde has made regular visits to the airport and whenever one takes place huge crowds still come to see this magnificent and graceful airliner.

One important event to take place during 1986, that would not only affect Leeds Bradford, but all U.K. airports, was the Airport Act (1986) which stipulated that all airports with a turnover in excess of £1 million owned by local authorities had to be formed into a limited company.

As a result of the Act, in April 1987 Leeds Bradford Airport Ltd. commenced trading. Shares for the new company are wholly owned by the five district Councils in West Yorkshire, Leeds and Bradford each holding 40%, while Calderdale, Kirklees and Wakefield hold 20%.

Being under a new company, at least in name, did not alter the day-to-day running of the airport. 1987 turned out to be another record year for both passengers and aircraft movements.

On the 25th January British Midland introduced its new livery to Leeds Bradford, to be followed on 27th March by its prestige Diamond Service on its five daily flights to London Heathrow.

Not to let foreign airlines get all the prestige, British Airways' Concorde G-BOAE made an appearance on 24th April. Again it attracted a huge crowd, as did Virgin Atlantic Boeing 747 which on 11th June made a Gatwick to Leeds Bradford flight. At the time a number of onlookers thought that Virgin was interested in transatlantic flights from the airport, but it was not to be. This was only a training flight.

However the transatlantic flights to Canada continued throughout 1987 operated by Wardair 747 via Birmingham, and for a short period they were joined by Worldways using either

Lockheed Tristar or Douglas DC8 Srs.63. Unfortunately Worldways did not seem to attract passengers in the same numbers as Wardair and after a brief summer season withdrew the flight.

On the 3rd May 1987 Leeds Bradford had its first visit by the superbly quiet Boeing 757 powered by two Rolls Royce RB 211 engines, when the all-white with red and gold cheat lines of Air 2000 made the first of what was to be a regular Sunday charter flight to Faro on behalf of Arrowsmith. Since then the airport has been host to a number of Boeing 757 flights operated by a variety of airlines such as Air Europe, Monarch, Hispania and recently Odyssey International.

Pop-stars have also drawn a lot of attention to the airport. On 15th August 1987 Rombac One-Eleven YR-BRF, on lease to London Express, brought Madonna to Leeds for her concert at Roundhay Park amongst tighter security than when one of the Queen's Flight aircraft visits.

By 1987 Brown Air had added Cardiff to their growing route network, but had decided to drop the Continental services and concentrate on the domestic market. Foreseeing the potential growth in the domestic sector, Brown Air placed an order for the new 39 seater Short 3.60 Srs.300 and became the U.K. launch customer for the type. The new aircraft G-BNDM was put in service on 12th October 1987. At the same time the airline adopted a new name and livery, and Capital Airlines came into being.

During the Winter months of 87/88 the new foreign departure lounge extension came into use. This doubled the size of the original lounge which had caused considerable problems in the past especially when there were several flights awaiting to board at the same time.

With the new runway extension, the airport was geared for the 'Nineties, but there was one stumbling block which prevented it competing successfully with other airports, and that was the operating hours. Schedule flights were not hindered by the 0700-2200 operating times, but it did deter a number of airlines and tour operators from flying from Leeds Bradford. Therefore an extension of the flying hours from 2200-0100, and resumption at 0600 am, was submitted for approval. After an eleven-day Public Inquiry in June 1987, the final decision was not made by the Secretary of State until 1989. The result of the delay caused T.N.T. which at the time was extremely interested in using the airport as a Northern base for their freight operations to choose Liverpool, and Leeds Bradford missed out once again as it did in earlier years. Today T.N.T. ultra quiet BAc 146 are used in regular night freight services throughout Europe from a number of regional airports in the U.K.

Although 1988 proved to be a very successful year for Leeds Bradford, holiday charter passengers figures dropped by 18% on the previous year. There was a sharp increase in schedule service passengers, however, mostly due to Capital Airlines acquiring new routes.

During May 1988 British Airways Concordes G-BOAF and G-BOAD made two separate visits to the airport, one being an overnight stop. As usual huge crowds gathered to see these magnificent silver birds.

One sad event to occur during the year was Wardair's announcement that the 1988 summer season would be the last the airline would be operating from Leeds Bradford. It was not due to poor support as there had been consistently high seat sales from the airport since the beginning, but rather due to a general re-organisation of the airline in Canada which had decided to withdraw all summer flights from U.K. regional airports and concentrate on Gatwick and Manchester.

Total passenger figures for the period 88/89 were 739,270 an increase of nearly 10% over the previous year. During the period scheduled service passengers had risen by a spectacular 34% on the previous year to a total of 507,200. Although it was a superb figure for Leeds Bradford, there was room for further improvement if the airport was to reach other regional airport figures.

The year began with everyone still waiting for the Secretary of State's decision on the extended operating hours. The delay caused great concern to the Board as well as the staff. Holiday flights from the airport were down on previous years, but fortunately schedule services were on the increase.

The gap left by Wardair, when it withdrew its Toronto flight the previous year, was taken up by a new Canadian airline —Odyssey International. This new carrier operated a weekly direct service to Toronto using the quiet Rolls Royce powered Boeing 757, and throughout the season became renowned for its punctuality and high standards.

Aer Lingus, Air U.K., British Midland and Capital still provided the airport with its regular schedule flights and were to remain the main operators at Leeds Bradford Airport. Although Aer Lingus had increased its Dublin frequency to twenty-one flights a week Capital insisted there was room for another carrier on the route. During the year, it introduced a twice-daily service to the Irish capital using Short 3.60 and for the first time since the 'Sixties Aer Lingus had some competition on the route.

There was also some rivalry on the Belfast service, between Capital and this time Air U.K. Here the situation was rather different as Air U.K. used Belfast Aldergrove while Capital used

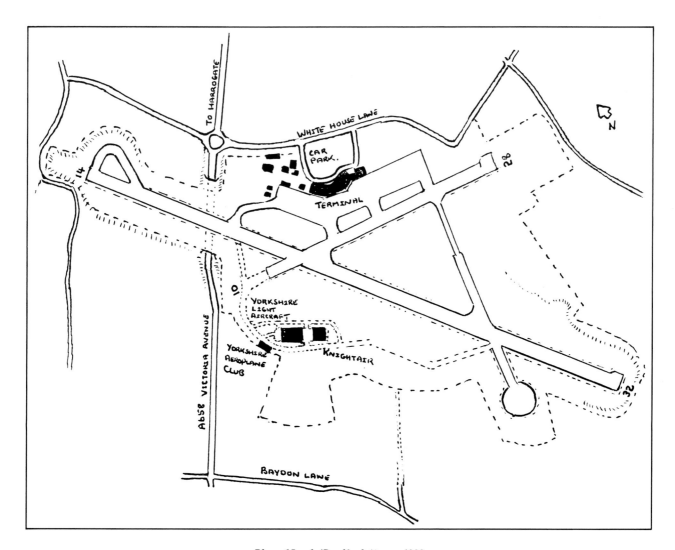

Plan of Leeds/Bradford Airport 1988.

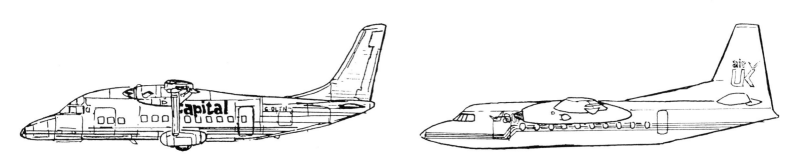

Shorts SD 360-300srs.

Fokker F27 Friendship.

British Midland Viscount in the airline's new livery.
Photograph courtesy of L. Woad.

An Air UK Fokker F27 landing after a flight from Amsterdam.
Photograph courtesy of L. Woad.

On 30th March 1984 Aer Lingus introduced the Short 360 commuter airline to Leeds Bradford Airport. Photograph courtesy of Aer Lingus.

British Airtours Lockheed Tristar resting on the edge of runway 14/32 after a mishap on 27th May 1985.

Belfast Harbour Airport, both companies claiming substantial increases on each route, which could only mean good news for Leeds Bradford.

During the year one observed the continuing expansion of Capital Airlines. To date the company operated a flexible fleet of aircraft comprising six Short 3.60 and two BAe 146 Srs.200 on various domestic and international routes not only from Leeds Bradford but from other regional airports. So within a very short period the airline has become a true national airline rather than regional. Let us hope that it does not lose its Yorkshire origins.

Throughout 1989 passengers handled at the airport rose dramatically especially during the summer months, one of the best being July when a total of 34,572 passengers was recorded —a massive 307% increase on July 1988. August was better still, 2411 aircraft movements occurred a 19% increase. So during the first eight months of the year nearly 600,000 passengers were handled, a 27% increase on the same period the previous year. Predictions of a million passengers looked very realistic.

The year produced its usual flight delays, which meant a number of angry stranded holiday-makers. But fortunately for Leeds Bradford there were very few. The biggest problem experienced at the airport was the collapse of the Spanish airline, Hispania, which had been a regular visitor to the airport for a number of years. On the 14th and 15th July two of its aircraft a Boeing 737.300 and a Boeing 757 were impounded by the authorities, as were the airline's other aircraft at Cardiff, Manchester, Teesside and Birmingham. Although thousands of holiday-makers were stranded at various destinations, the tour companies within a short period found alternative carriers. As a result Leeds Bradford was host to a number of new airlines and their equipment.

During the 'Eighties the airport had attracted a number of private aircraft, especially executive types. Yorkshire Light Aircraft since its early days has been the centre of private flying at the airport. As well as providing hangar space and maintenance facilities, it still holds the Avgas franchise for the airport. In 1989 it became an appointed agent and service-centre for the American Mooney Company.

Recently Yorkshire Light Aircraft's hangar became the base for the first two Beechcroft 400 executive jets in the country, one owned by Bass PLC. (G-BRBZ) while the other still in its U.S. registration N 15858 owned by Ogdens. Other aircraft maintained by Y.L.A. are Mountleigh Citatlon 111, Elliotts Bricks, Citation 11 and Asda's Beech 200 Super King Air.

Finally in August 1989 the Secretary of State gave his decision on L.B.A's request for an extension of operating hours. The 0600 — 0100 was rejected in favour of retaining the current 0700 opening, but extended the evening operation from 2200 — 2330. The extra ninety minutes would only be of marginal use to the charter airlines as the tour operators wanted to fly three round trips over a 24 hour period. So once again the airport lost the opportunity for an airline to base one of its aircraft at the airport. There was one concession however. The airport could remain open until 0100 to cater for an incoming flight, but there would be no take-off permitted after 2330. Within days the airport authority re-submitted its application, knowing if the investigation took as long as the previous one, it would be well into the 'Nineties before any results would be published.

The decade saw a gigantic transformation of Leeds Bradford Airport, making it into a major International Airport capable of handling any aircraft. A new extended runway became operational, and a new modernised terminal capable of handling over a million passengers a year, with a modest extension in operating hours. Completely new routes appeared as well as an increase in the frequency of existing ones.

The 'Eighties as well as introducing new airlines to the airport, brought a new generation of jet liners like the B737-300-400 Srs. B757, B747 Jumbo Jet, the Tristar, Airbus A310 and A320 MD83, and of course the most prestigious airliner of all — the Concorde. So without any hesitation it can be stated that the 'Eighties was quite a remarkable decade.

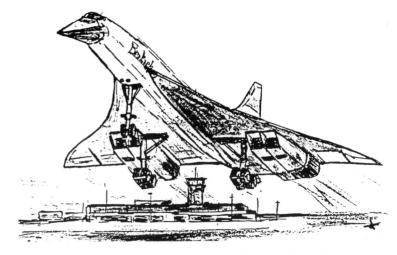

A British Airways Concorde taking off from Leeds/Bradford.

Genair Short 330 commenced a Leeds – Gatwick service in 1982.
Photograph courtesy of MAP.

In the early 'Eighties Air Malta Boeing 707 were frequently used on their I.T. charter flights to the Island of Malta.

Dan Air Boeing 737-200 taking off on a charter flight to Palma on behalf of Intasun. Photograph courtesy of Dan Air.

British Airways Concorde at Leeds Bradford Airport – each time this magnificent aircraft appears at the airport, it still draws thousands of sightseers.

*During the 1988 summer season
British Air Ferries Viscounts were
used on charter flights to Jersey.
Photograph courtesy of L. Woad.*

*The Spanish airline Spantax
Boeing 737 landing.*

Leeds Bradford Airport's own airline Brown Air – Gulfstream G-BRWN taxi-ing.
Photograph courtesy of L. Woad.

Passengers disembarking from Dan Air Boeing 737.

General view of the airport's new terminal which was officially opened on 18th July 1985.

Wardair Boeing 747 Jumbo Jet landing on its first transatlantic flight.

York Races has attracted a number of charters to Leeds Bradford Airport. Photo shows a Hapag-Lloyd Boeing 727 on one such visit.

An apron is a hive of activity. Here a Britannia Airways Boeing 737 is being tended by a catering vehicle, a refueller as well as by the baggage handler.

Hispania Boeing 757 were impounded at Leeds Bradford Airport when the airline ceased operations in July 1989.

An Air UK F27 landing at dusk.

During the 'Eighties, British Midland replaced their Viscount with Douglas DC9 jetliners.

Another view of Concorde.

Concorde viewed from the building interior.

Two Britannia Airways Boeing 737-200s being prepared for their next flight.

An unusual view of the airport's apron through a window of a taxi-ing aircraft.

Capital Airlines Short 360 were a common sight at Leeds Bradford Airport during the 'Eighties.

British Airtours Boeing 737 were used on I.T. flights from the airport.

General view of the Yorkshire Light Aircraft hangar with various aircraft parked in the foreground.

A rare visitor to the airport was this United Arab Emirates Boeing 707 on a cargo flight.
Photograph courtesy of L. Woad.

Accidents are very rare at Leeds Bradford Airport; but during a snow storm in January 1980 a Cessna 402 overshot runway 14/32 on to the Harrogate Road. Remarkably the pilot walked away safely.
Photograph courtesy of C. Walker.

TODAY AND THE FUTURE

As one entered the last decade in the present century, Leeds Bradford Airport still had not reached its millionth passenger mark, which it had worked so hard to achieve by its sixtieth anniversary in 1991.

Throughout the summer month of 1989 total passenger figures looked extremely promising and at the time everyone thought that the airport could boast of handling a million passengers by the end of the year. However, due mostly to a reduction in holiday charter flights, the total figure only reached 889,736, but it was still a record for Leeds Bradford Airport. Total aircraft movements for the same period were 56,827, nearly six thousand movements more than the previous year.

The 'Nineties will doubtless be a record decade both in finance and movements, but it will also be the most expensive period. As expected, the E.C. continues with market unification proposals, which meant the disappearance of all duty-free trade between E.C. countries by 1992. The majority of regional airports will find some difficulties ahead, as at the moment large revenues are obtained from such sales. The gap left by this will have to be replaced by other sources of income, such as renting shop spaces in the terminal area like one sees at some international airports. A good example is of course Gatwick village.

1992 also meant de-regulation, which should benefit Leeds Bradford with much new business, but are the airport and the airlines using it ready for this important change? Unless Leeds Bradford Airport gets the investment to carry out the proposed improvements and new buildings, as well as unrestricted operating hours, it will lose out once again. Up to the time of writing Leeds Bradford Airport has not attracted any foreign scheduled airlines, especially the Continental ones. In the very near future one could see names like the German regional airlines D.L.T. or the French T.A.T., Netherlines, Sabena or even S.A.S. being regular visitors in the 'Nineties.

Another Government directive that could be a great burden on the airport's finances will be major changes in the airport's security service, including acquiring new super sensitive baggage X-ray machines capable of tracing most explosive substances.

An ambitious multi-million pound programme of expansion and improvements that was planned to be completed by 1990 will no doubt be completed during the present decade, although some of the planned improvements have already been completed, including the £1.5 million extension to the parking apron and a new £.5 million freight transit facilities. There have also been substantial refurbishing of the restaurant and bar areas of the terminal building.

Other improvements planned are the construction of new domestic arrival and departure facilities with an extended restaurant as well as three floors of office space, which at the moment is non-existent. This new domestic terminal is long-overdue as the present arrangements are very unsatisfactory and in theory after 1992 travellers to E.C. countries would be classed as domestic passengers. Therefore the present terminal needs considerable modifications to separate foreign and domestic passengers.

Also planned is a large engineering hangar adjoining the recently completed apron, and another two smaller hangars plus an exceextive hangar situated on the south side of the airport near Northair and Y.L.A. It will be interesting to see if these facilities will attract any aircraft servicing organisation to the airport.

There is also an upgrading of the radar installation planned as well as the installation of a new high-technology approach radar system, and before the end of the decade a new instrument landing system will be in operation suitable for aircraft landing in nil visibility.

Other improvements included in this 60 million pound investment are upgrading the fire stations and equipment, improving the taxiway, and building a new flight catering commissary.

Also proposed is a new 150 room four-star airport hotel, to be built opposite the passenger terminal and car parks.

The future looks extremely promising although at the time of writing there seems to be a reduction in holiday I.T. charter flights from the airport. This is the result of a general reduction nationwide in holidays to the Mediterranean regions. At the moment further-afield destinations to the Far East, Australia and especially Florida seem to be popular with the holiday-maker. And what a wonderful bonus for the airport if weekly transatlantic services to New York and Orlando were to become a reality.

If the outlook for holiday traffic is less rosy, schedule services look healthier and will be the major source of revenue for the airport in the 'Nineties. Most of the airlines like Aer Lingus, Air U.K., and British Midland have geared themselves for de-regulation in 1992 and were ready to meet this important event.

Alas 1990 proved to be a fateful year for the Yorkshire success story Capital Airlines, when in June it ceased operations.

Whatever the actual cause of this collapse was, it certainly created some shock waves, not only throughout the airline world, but especially at Leeds Bradford Airport. As with the disappearance of Capital, the airport lost a major source of revenue and business which it could ill afford at a time when there were major expansion plans in the pipeline. Happily at the time of writing there are plans to re-start the airline with a reduced fleet of Short 360 and a smaller route network. At the moment the Glasgow service has been taken over temporarily by Loganair using their Short 360, but they have applied to the C.A.A. for a permanent licence for the route. Also in the wings are other airlines like Air Europe Express, Gill Aviation and Jersey European who are waiting to pick up some of the other Capital routes.

The other major event in the airport calendar at the start of the decade came in November 1990 when a twice-daily service to Brussels was operated by Sabena subsidiary D.A.T. using a 29 seater Embraer Brazilia.

With the collapse of Capital Airlines in June 1990, there were several attempts to start a Yorkshire based airline. One of these was Yorkshire European Airways equipped with two 14-seater Bandeirante commuter airliners, providing the airport with air links to Southampton and Aberdeen, but sadly on 22nd November 1993 the company ceased operations. However during the following year a new airline emerged Knightair, which took over Y.E.A. routes as well as adding week-day services to the Isle of Man. Other airlines to make their debut at Leeds Bradford were A.T.S. Vulcan, Eurodirect and British Airways Express, formerly City Flyer Express who took over the Gatwick flights.

While new airlines were emerging, old well-known names were disappearing like Dan Air which was in serious financial difficulties and ceased operations on 23rd October 1993.

However during 1994, Manx Airlines, who had taken over all Loganair schedule flights outside Scotland increased their frequencies on their flight to Glasgow from Leeds, and for the first time introduced the Jetstream J41 and B.Ae A.T.P. to the airport.

It was also during 1994 that Mr. Gordon Dennison retired as Airport Director and was replaced by Mr. Bill Savage.

With the airport in the middle of a multi-million investment to improve and modernise the terminal and upgrade other airport facilities, Mr. Savage's appointment to the directorship could not have happened at a more exciting time. Of course the best news the airport received during 1994 was its twenty-four hour operating licence which removed the stumbling block that prevented any additional investment and growth, so at last the airport's future looks rosey — white one of course!

Perhaps during the decade one will see T.N.T. freight service making Leeds Bradford Airport one of their bases and Datapost making use of the airport. Both would be most welcome.

However once all the alterations and improvements have been completed, they will ensure that Leeds Bradford Airport will hold its position as an international airport and serve the community and the area to the end of the century and beyond.

Although there are as many as nine check-in desks at the airport there are still some hold-ups during peak times; but there are plans to reposition the present desks to allow a smoother check-in.

An aerial view of the airport as it is today.
Photograph courtesy of Air Supply.

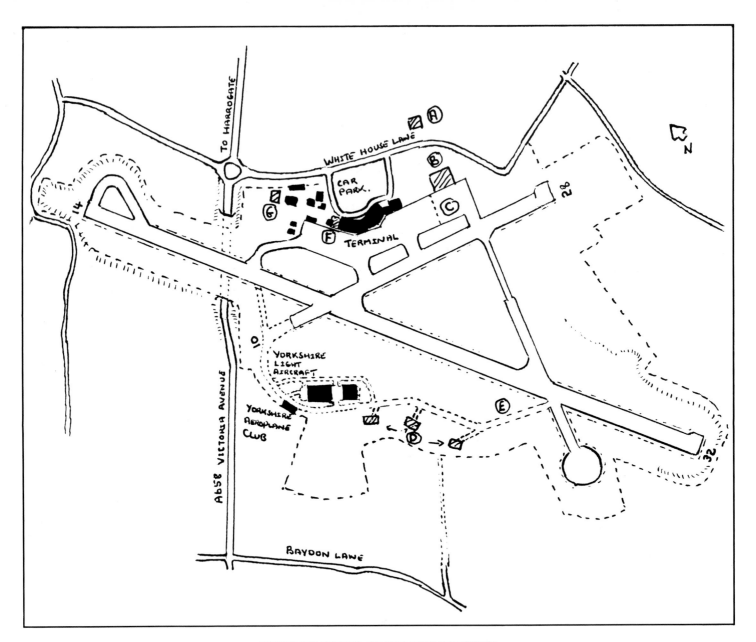

DEVELOPMENT PLAN FOR THE 'NINETIES

a. New 150 Bedroom hotel.
b. New engineering hangar.
c. Extended aircraft parking apron (already completed).
d. New engineering hangars and an executive hangar.

e. Upgrading existing taxiway.
f. A new domestic terminal with three floors of office space.
g. New freight transit shed (completed).

For the comfort of passengers two brand new Van Hool airport buses were acquired during 1990 for the transfer of passengers between terminal and aircraft.

A BAe Jetstream 31 demonstrator at Leeds Bradford recently. Could it be a foretaste of a new regional airline for the airport?

Duty-free and Tax-free sales made a valuable contribution to the airport's income, but after 1992 alterna revenue had to be found.

The refurbished second floor dining area. Note the Philippa Threlfall mural creation on the right side wall.

A touch of nostalgia came to Leeds Bradford Airport in July 1991, when an Air Atlantique Douglas C47 Dakota gave joyrides. Photo shows passengers about to embark from a 1950 vintage Bedford Coach with a Dan Air B.A.C. One-Eleven taxi-ing in the background.

One of the airport's crash tenders, a vast improvement compared to the emergency vehicles of the 'Fifties.

Passengers disembarking from a Jersey European Fokker F27 flight JY733 from Belfast.

During 1991 Aspro Travel made its northern headquarters at the airport, and the Company's own airline Inter European Airways became a common sight.

SCHEDULED AIRLINES
THAT HAVE USED THE AIRPORT

Aer Lingus ☘

The Irish national airline operates scheduled services to all parts of the world from Dublin. It was formed in 1936 to provide an air service between points in Ireland and Great Britain. Aer Lingus began schedule flights to Leeds Bradford in 1960, at first in partnership with B.K.S. Air Transport using Douglas C47 Dakotas.

In 1962 the Irish airline was the first to use Turbo prop aircraft to Leeds Bradford, followed some years later by another first with pure jet equipment, a BAC 1-11 and Boeing 737. In 1984 Aer Lingus Commuter was formed to operate services to U.K. regional airports, so to date the airline uses Short 3.60 and occasionally the new Fokker 50 on the Leeds flights.

AirUK

Air U.K. was formed on 1st January 1980, when Air Anglia, British Island Airways (not connected with the present B.I.A.), Air West and Air Wales merged into a single entity. Only some years earlier, several well-known airlines such as Jersey Airways, Manx Airlines and Silver City, two of which were well known at Leeds Bradford were merged to become British Island Airways.

Air Anglia had been formed in 1970 by the merger of Norfolk Airways and Anglia Air Charter, and had been providing Leeds Bradford airport with schedule flights since 1974.

Today Air U.K. is Britain's third largest schedule airline providing air service to and from airports in the British Isles. It has been one of the major airlines operating out of Leeds Bradford airport for some years with regular daily flights to Aberdeen, Belfast, Edinburgh, Glasgow and Norwich, as well as international flights to Amsterdam. In recent years the airline has taken over the Guernsey flights from Dan Air and due to increased traffic has increased the frequency.

During the 'Eighties Air U.K. took delivery of five BAe. 146 Srs.200 and 300. These superbly quiet airliners are used on the newly acquired London (Gatwick) services to both Edinburgh and Glasgow. It will be interesting to see whether this type will eventually replace the airline fleets of Fokkers F27's.

Aircraft used by the airline at Leeds Bradford are Fokker F27 although during the latter part of 1989 the BAe.146 were introduced on the Amsterdam service.

British Midland first appeared at Leeds Bradford airport in the livery of Derby Airways in the early 'Sixties, when they began a Derby-Leeds-Glasgow service using a Douglas C47 Dakota.

The airline's origins go back to 1938 when Air Schools Ltd. was formed, specialising in flying instruction for R.A.F. pilots. In 1949 the air school became Derby Aviation and Wolverhampton Aviation with bases at Buneston and Wolverhampton and were involved in *ad hoc* passenger and cargo charters using de Havilland Rapides. 1959 saw the airline changing its name to Derby Airways and eventually to British Midland in 1964.

The early flights from Leeds were short-lived. It was not until 1979 that British Midland next appeared at the airport, when it acquired the London, Heathrow flights from British Airways, which it has kept ever since. At first B.M.A used Viscounts and Fokker F27, to be eventually replaced by Douglas DC9, although there was a brief appearance of the A.T.P. in the 'Eighties.

Today British Midland operates a five times daily jet Diamond Service to the capital city, so providing Leeds Bradford with a busy prestige connection.

In 1987, Airline of Britain Holdings was formed to oversee the running of British Midland and its subsidiaries, Loganair, Manx Airways and London City Airways. Under the superb managership of Mr. Michael Bishop, British Midland has become one of the major schedule operators in the British Isles.

B.Ae 146 belonging to Air U.K.

British Midland Douglas DC9 are used on the London Heathrow flights.

110

*For a brief period during 1990
B.M.A. used its newly acquired
Boeing 737-300 on the London flights.*

*Capital Short SD360 had become a
common sight at the airport, but sadly
this Leeds based airline ceased
operations in 1990, a great loss to the
airport and the community.*

Capital

The airline commenced operations at Leeds Bradford airport during 1983 as Brown Air, part of the Brown Group of Companies. At first a general air taxi service was undertaken until a Leeds-Oslo schedule service using a Cessna 441 Conquest began on 1st October 1984. Soon afterwards, further services operated to Frankfurt and Humberside.

In January 1986 the company purchased a Dart powered Gruman Gulfstream, which doubled the airline capacity.

When Metropolitan Airways ceased operations in August 1985, the Cardiff and Glasgow service became available and it was not long before Brown Air saw the potential of these two routes and decided to take them over.

Foreseeing the potential growth of the newly acquired service the airline ordered new 39 seater Short 360 Srs.300, but while awaiting delivery, leased a Short 330 and disposed of the Gulfstream. The new aircraft were put into service in October 1987, at the same time as the airline adopted its present name and livery.

Capital not only served Cardiff and Glasgow, but also Bristol, Belfast, Dublin and London Gatwick were added to the ever growing schedule routes from Leeds Bradford as well as international flights to Jersey, Dublin and Brussels. Also Capital connected Belfast and Luton and Cardiff with Jersey.

Following the introduction of two BAe. 146 Srs.200 in late 1989, Capital provided Leeds Bradford with services to the Mediterranean holiday destinations.

So within a mere seven years this Yorkshire-based airline had become one of the main commuter airline in the United Kingdom, its Short 360 becoming a common sight at most British airports especially at Leeds Bradford. However in June 1990 Capital Airlines ceased operations due to financial problems with its parent company.

DAN-AIR

Dan Air began operations on 21st May 1953, by Davies and Newman, from which its name derived.

At first the airline was only involved with *ad hoc* charters, mainly from Blackbushe, but in 1956 its first schedule flight to Jersey took place and from then Dan Air was the major Channel Island operator.

Dan Air's first association with Leeds Bradford was in the early 'Seventies when it took over the Glasgow flights from British Midland, and it was the first airline to introduce the French built Nord 262 turbo prop to the airport. Soon afterwards Dan Air began a schedule service to Bristol and Cardiff using the newly acquired H.S. 748, followed in 1978 by a schedule service to Jersey, which still operates today.

In 1984 Dan Air helped to form Metropolitan Airways with a view to providing an airline feeder service to central points. This new airline took over the Glasgow, Cardiff and Bristol routes using a Short 330, but the following year it ceased operation, and Dan Air was not prepared to take them over. Dan Air's only connection with Leeds Bradford in recent years was its weekend Jersey flights using BAC 1-11 and BAe 146, although Dan Air's Boeing 727, 737 and B.A.C One-Eleven were regular visitors on the I.T. flights to holiday destinations. However due to financial problems the airline ceased operations on 23rd October 1992 and its aircraft and most of its routes were taken over by British Airways.

LOGANAIR

When Capital Airlines ceased operations in June 1990 a considerable number of valuable routes became available, one being the Glasgow route which was temporarily taken over by Loganair. Eventually on the 28th October 1990, this Scottish airline was awarded a permanent Licence for the route and today its Short 360 provides three flights daily to Glasgow.

Loganair was formed on 1st February 1962 and provides a comprehensive regional passenger schedule service throughout Scotland centred on Glasgow and Edinburgh. Recently services from Manchester have been added to the airliner's network.

Until recently the airline was part of the Airlines of Britain Group providing a feeder service to British Midland's schedule with its varied fleet of aircraft. However during the last two years the airline has had some financial problems, and as a result all Loganair routes from Manchester and Leeds were taken over by its sister airline Manx Airways. In September 1994 the airline was taken over by British Airways Express.

JERSEY EUROPEAN

A new airline to Leeds Bradford Airport appeared on 25th March 1991 when Jersey European began three flights daily to Belfast City using their Fokker F27 — a route left vacant when Capital Airlines ceased operations. The airline also provides the airport with weekend flights to Jersey.

Jersey European Airways was formed in November 1979 after the take-over of the Jersey based Intra Airways operations. In November 1983 the airline was acquired by the Walker Steel Group who already owned Spacegrand Aviation. Finally on 26th October 1985 the two airlines were amalgamated.

Today Jersey European fleet consists of Fokker F27, Short 360 and D.H.C. Twin Otters.

Manx Airlines began operations on 1st November 1982, when British Midland and the British and Commonwealth Shipping Co. (through Air U.K.) formed an airline to serve the Isle of Man and points on the mainland. Today Manx has a regular schedule service from Ronaldsway to London Heathrow, Manchester, Blackpool, Belfast City, Dublin, Jersey, Liverpool and Glasgow, with weekend services to Birmingham, Bristol, Newcastle, Leeds Bradford and Edinburgh.

Until recently Manx provided a schedule link between Liverpool and Heathrow, but has been taken over by its parent company British Midland.

Manx Airlines has provided weekend flights between the Isle of Man and Leeds for a number of years using a Short 360, and perhaps with an increase in traffic one will see their ATP being put on the route.

Today Manx Airlines is part of the Airlines of Britain Group with a modern fleet of BAe 146, BAe ATP and Short 360.

Aer Lingus Short 360 – the Irish national airline
has been providing Yorkshire with an airlink
with Dublin since 1960.

*Dan Air B.Ae 146 were used
on weekend flights to Jersey.*

*A new airline to Leeds Bradford Airport
is Jersey European. Its Fokker F27 are
used on daily flights to Belfast and
weekend flights to Jersey.*

A Jersey European advert of the 'Nineties.

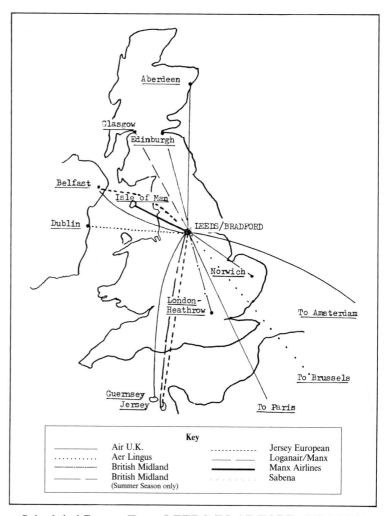

Scheduled Routes From LEEDS/BRADFORD AIRPORT.

MAJOR INCLUSIVE TOUR AIRLINES USING LEEDS BRADFORD AIRPORT

ADRIA

Adria operated charter services between Yugoslavia and Leeds Bradford for Yugotours. Equipment mostly seen at the airport were DC9's although lately MD 81 and MD 82 were put on the routes and during the summer of 1989, an Airbus was seen quite often at Leeds Bradford Airport. Due to the civil war in Yugoslavia the airline ceased operations in 1993.

AEROMARITIME

This French airline which is a subsidiary of U.T.A. operates passengers and cargo charter flights. Its Boeing 737-300 were seen for the first time at Leeds Bradford during the summer of 1989 filling in gaps made by the disappearance of Hispania.

AIR EUROPA

The airline was set up in June 1986 with 25 per cent of the shares owned by International Leisure Group. The livery is very similar to Air Europe. Therefore there is considerable exchange of aircraft. Air Europa flights are usually to points on the Spanish mainline for its main customer I.L.G. Travel.

AIR EUROPE

Air Europe was wholly owned by I.L.G. It was formed in July 1978 and commenced operations in May 1979.

The airline was only involved with I.T. flights but with the acquiring of schedule flights to Paris and Brussels and the taking over of Connectair, Air Europe became a major airline in Europe.

Nearly all of Air Europe flights were for Intasun, Lancaster and Global holidays with destinations to various parts around the Mediterranean. In 1989 Air Europe's aircraft seen at Leeds Bradford were Boeing 737-300, but their 757-200 occasionally made a brief appearance. Sadly in April 1991 Air Europe and ILG ceased operations.

AIR MALTA

For a number of years, Air Malta has been flying holiday makers to Malta from Leeds Bradford Airport, again mostly for Intasun. Aircraft used are mostly Boeing 737-200, but on a few occasions the airline has used their Boeing 720B.

AIR 2000

The airline began operations in April 1987 using Boeing 757-200 on charter flights from Manchester and Glasgow on behalf of Owners Abroad Group, its parent company. The airline is not a regular visitor to Leeds Bradford Airport, but when it does come its startling livery catches everyone's attention. Air 2000's first appearance at the airport was in 1987, on the Faro flights for Arrowsmith.

AIRTOURS INTERNATIONAL

Although this new airline was only formed in 1990 by its parent company Airtours Holidays, within a short time its fleet had increased to ten MD 83's. In 1993 it took over the Cardiff-based holiday group Aspro Travel Ltd. as well as its airline Inter European Airways which had been a common sight at Leeds and Bradford for some years. As from 1994 Airtours A320 and MD 83 continued holiday flights on behalf of Airtours Holidays and Aspro to various destinations from the airport.

AIR TRANSAT

This newly formed Canadian charter airline is based at Montreal. During 1989 Leeds Bradford was fortunate to be host to its tristar on a number of occasions when it stood in for Odyssey International.

AIR U.K. LEISURE

This is one of the newer airlines to be seen at Leeds Bradford Airport. It is a sister company to Air U.K. and began holiday flights in April 1988.

The major shareholders are Air U.K., Bricom Group and Viking International. Its first appearance at Leeds Bradford Airport was during the summer of 1989 when its Boeing 737-400 Srs. was used on I.T. flights to Malaga on behalf of Intasun.

AVIACO

Aviaco is a major Spanish domestic airline and a subsidiary of Iberia. The airline has appeared from time to time at Leeds Bradford on I.T. flights, mostly to Tenerife using their DC 9's.

AVIOGENEX

This airline was mostly used for passenger charter flights to points in Europe and Mediterranean area from Yugoslavia, in association with Yugotours.

Aviogenex was a regular visitor at Leeds Bradford Airport for some years on flights to Dubrovnick using a Boeing 737-200 or a Tupolev TU 134A. Like Adria it ceased operations due to the civil war in Yugoslavia.

BALKAN

This government owned airline operates charter flights from points in Bulgaria to most European cities. Flights from Leeds Bradford are to Varna using Tupolev TU154.

BRITANNIA AIRWAYS

Britannia began trading as Euravia Ltd. on 1st December 1961 with three ex- EL AL Lockheed LO49 Constellation. Another three aircraft belonging to Skyways were later added to the airline's fast-growing fleet. By 1964 Euravia had become one of the leading holiday charter airlines in the country and there was an urgent need for more modern equipment. The most logical choice was Bristol Britannia, on offer from B.O.A.C. In all, ten of these turbo props were acquired and in honour of the new aircraft the company changed its name to Britannia Airways.

In 1965 the Thomson Organisation took over both Universal Sky Tours and Britannia Airways. As a result, Thomson Holidays was formed. With the coming of the jet age Britannia was not going to be left out, placing an order with Boeing for 737's, the first G-AURL being received on 8th July 1968.

Britannia's Boeing 737 made its first appearance at Leeds Bradford Airport in 1976 and from that day it has been the main holiday charter airline operating at the airport.

During the winter months one of Britannia's 737's is permanently based at the airport.

Today Britannia Airways is Britain's second largest airline and the largest charter carrier in the world operating from nearly every regional airport in the U.K. In August 1988 the Thomson Organisation took over Horizon Holidays and its associated airline Orion Airways. Its fleet comprises of Boeing 757-200 Srs., and Boeing 767 which has only once been seen at Leeds Bradford Airport.

BRITISH AIRWAYS

Although British Airways is not a regular visitor to the airport as such, its chartered Concorde has delighted all concerned with its rare visits to the airport over the years.

Until recently its subsidiary British Airtours was a regular visitor, flying I.T. flights for the major tour operators, using mostly Boeing 737 with the occasional Tristar until the incident in 1985.

With the acquisition of British Caledonian Airways in December 1987, the name British Airtours was dropped in favour of Caledonian Airways, and all I.T. flights were made by the new airline.

BRITISH ISLAND AIRWAYS

Up until January 1990 British Island provided charter services from the U.K. to holiday destinations in Europe and North Africa. Formerly part of the British and Commonwealth Shipping Group, it became an independent airline on 1st April 1982 and during 1986 was the first British airline to be publicly quoted on the stock exchange.

The airline's BAe 1-11 500 Srs. and MD 83 provided Leeds Bradford with its weekly holiday charter to Mahon, Minorca from 1986. During 1989 the airline got into financial difficulties, and after several unsuccessful attempts to save it British Island finally ceased operations in February 1990.

HISPANIA

Hispania was a regular visitor to Leeds Bradford Airport until it ceased operations in July 1989. Its fleet of Boeing 737-200 300 Srs. and 757 operated I.T. flights from the airport to Palma and Malaga mostly for Intasun and Thomson. Its brightly painted aircraft will be sadly missed from the airport.

JAT — YUGOSLAVIA AIRLINES

The above was a wholly state-owned airline, operating an extensive network of both schedule and I.T. flights and was founded in 1947. Due to the civil war in Yugoslavia, the airline ceased operations.

MIDDLE EAST AIRLINE (MEA)

Not a regular visitor to Leeds Bradford Airport, but in recent years several of its Boeing 707-320c have been sub-leased to various airlines on holiday flights.

MONARCH AIRLINE

This U.K. carrier operates inclusive tour flights only. It was formed in 1967 with its first charter flight on 5th April 1968 using a Bristol Britannia from Luton to Madrid. As business gradually increased the airline acquired its first jet equipment the BAC 1-11, but today Monarch operates the latest airliners, like the Boeing 737-300, Boeing 757-200 and the Airbus A300-600R.

Nearly half the airline's business is provided by its sister company Cosmos Holidays. Cosmos withdrew all holiday flights from Leeds, but up to 1987 Monarch aircraft were regular visitors at the airport, when operating for Thomson on their Alicante flights.

OASIS AIRLINES INTERNATIONAL

This new Spanish airline formerly known as Andalusair only appeared on the charter scene in 1988, and made its first appearance at Leeds Bradford Airport in the summer of 1989 when its MD 83 stood in for Air U.K. Leisure 737-400 during their operating difficulties.

ODYSSEY INTERNATIONAL

Another newly formed international airline that made its first appearance at Leeds Bradford Airport during the summer of 1989. Its Boeing 757 operated a weekly flight to Toronto, providing the airport and the area with important international transatlantic flights. In 1992 the airline ceased operations. All Canadian flights were taken over by Air Transat.

RYAN AIR

This independent Irish carrier was a leader in the introduction of low economy scheduled services between points in Ireland and the U.K. Its Rombac One-Eleven can be seen in most British airports.

In 1989 Ryan Air made its first appearance at Leeds Bradford Airport, operating a seasonal flight to Connaught in Ireland.

SPANAIR

This was another new Spanish airline to appear at Leeds Bradford Airport during the summer of 1989. Its MD 83 operated holiday flights to Tenerife.

WARDAIR

This Canadian airline dates back to 1946 when Maxwell W. Ward began a bush operation in Canada. Today it has grown into one of the largest Canadian airlines with a service network not only covering North America, but also Europe and Central America. Wardair Boeing 747 Jumbo jets first appeared at Leeds Bradford Airport during the summer of 1986 when a weekly transatlantic flight to Toronto via Birmingham was started. But due to re-organisation at home — a take-over of Wardair by P. W. A. Corps. — Scheduled flights to Britain's regional airports ceased in 1988.

WORLDWAYS CANADA

This Canadian passenger charter airline provided world-wide charters using either DC 8 Srs. 63 or Lockheed L1011 Tristars. Worldways made a brief appearance during 1987, but unfortunately did not attract as many passengers as Wardair.

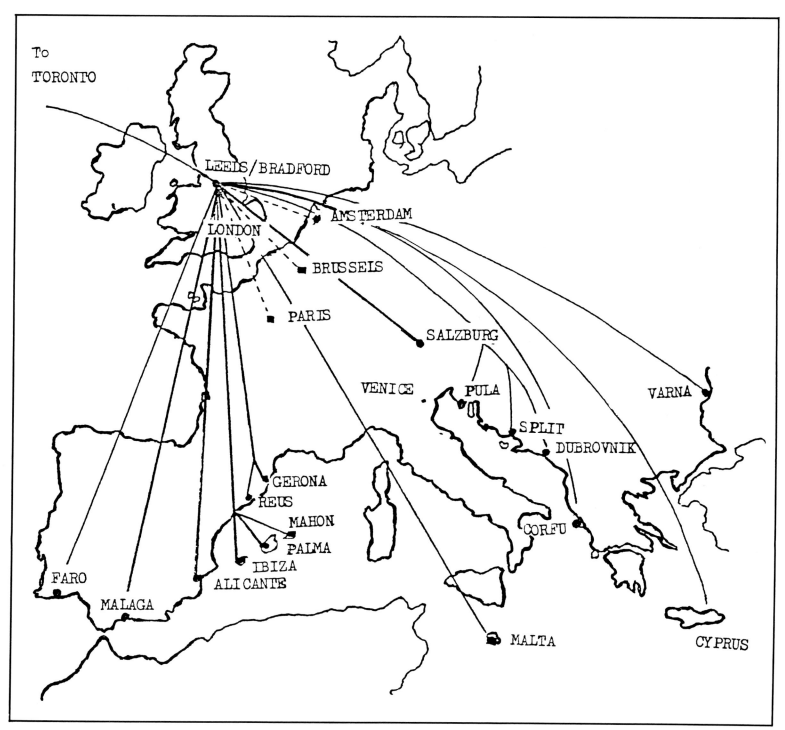

Inclusive Tours Charters from Leeds/Bradford Airport.

119

Adria Rombac One Eleven used on holiday flights to Yugoslavia.

Air 2000 Boeing 757-200 was used on flights to Faro in 1987.

Air U.K. Leisure first used their Boeing 737-400 on flights to Palma during the 1991 summer season.

Aviaco Douglas DC9 about to take off on an extremely wet runway.

Another airline that served Yugoslavia from Leeds Bradford Airport was Aviogenex – photo shows a Boeing 737-200 taxi-ing.

Balkan Airways Tupolev TU 154A.

Since 1976 Britannia Airways Boeing 737-200 have been regular visitors to the airport.

An Hispania Boeing 737-300 about to take off – but sadly during 1990 the airline ceased operations.

A J.A.T. Yugoslav Airlines Boeing 727 during a rare visit to Yorkshire.

Middle East Airlines Boeing 707 has been used by various tour companies.

A Monarch Boeing 737-200.

Odyssey International Boeing 757 took over the Toronto flights from Wardair in 1988.

*A Wardair Boeing 747
Jumbo Jet about to land.*

*During a brief season in 1987
Worldways of Canada appeared
at Leeds Bradford Airport with
their Lockheed Tristar.*

No. 609 SQUADRON (WEST RIDING) ROYAL AUXILIARY FORCE

As mentioned previously, No. 609 Squadron had very close ties with the County of Yorkshire and in particular Yeadon Aerodrome, so much so that a memorial plaque was installed in the small aircraft viewing deck next to the airport's terminal. With re-development, the plaque was removed indoors and is now in a place of honour on the first floor spectators gallery.

The Squadron was formed as one of the Auxiliary Air Force units on 10th February 1936. For the next few years, like most other Auxiliary Squadrons, it was classed as a light bomber unit equipped with Hawker Harts, to be replaced by the more modern Hinds in 1938.

In December 1938 it was decided that No. 609 should become a fighter unit under the command of Sqd. Ldr. Ambler who remained with the Squadron until December 1939. The Hawker Hinds which by now had been converted to a fighter role were kept until 1939. A week before the outbreak of the Second World War the Squadron received its first modern fighters, the famous Vickers Supermarine Spitfire MK 1.

Yeadon had only a short glimpse of 609's new Spitfires, as the Squadron moved to Catterick in September 1939. Again their stay in Yorkshire was short-lived and before long the West Riding Squadron had become one of the R.A.F. units moving to Manston in Kent, where during the Battle of Britain they performed distinguished service.

In 1944 the Squadron reverted back to its light-bomber role,

when it was equipped with Hawker Typhoon 1b armed with bombs and rocket projectiles which became a formidable ground attack weapon causing havoc amongst enemy armour from 'D' Day onwards. For the rest of the war No. 609 kept its Typhoons until being disbanded at Wunsturf on the 15th September 1945.

Throughout its service life No. 609 Squadron could boast of having distinguished C.O.'s, one notable person being S/Ldr. R. P. "Rolly" Beaumont D.F.C. who after the war became chief test pilot for the English Electric Aircraft Company and had the honour of test flying Britain's first supersonic fighter, the legendary Lightning and later the remarkable T.S.R.2.

During 1946 the Royal Auxiliary Air Force Squadrons were reformed, and on 31st July, No. 609 West Riding Squadron arose once again at Yeadon, under the command of Sqd. Ldr. P. A. Womersley D.F.C. as a night fighter unit equipped with de Havilland Mosquito NF 30.

These Merlin-powered night fighters remained with No. 609 until 1948 when the Squadron was re-equipped with Spitfire LF 16e which at the time became the standard equipment of the Auxiliary Squadrons. The LF 16 remained with 609 until 1951, when the piston engine fighters gave way to the modern Gloster Meteor F8. As Yeadon was not suitable for jet operations, the Squadron moved to Church Fenton in October 1950 where, as well as their new equipment, they received a new Co. Sqd. Ldr. A. Hudson D.F.C..

During its stay at Church Fenton No. 609 attended summer camp at such varied locations as Tangmere, Thorney Island, Manston, Chivenor and Sylt and Celle on the continent, which were quite popular postings with the part-time pilots.

By the mid 'Fifties the writing was on the wall for the Auxiliary Squadron. It was a luxury that the country could not afford, and during 1956 and 1957 one saw the disappearance of all Auxiliary Air Force Squadrons including No. 609 in 1957.

SQUADRON CODES

Before the Second World War No. 609's code was BL, but by December 1939 the Squadron code had changed to PR which remained with the Squadron throughout the war until 1946.

In 1946 when reverting back to the Auxiliary Air Force, the Squadron code changed to R.A.P., until 1948 when all codes disappeared from all R.A.F. aircraft.

A BRIEF SUMMARY OF No. 609
WHILE STATIONED IN YORKSHIRE

10 February 1936: Formed at Yeadon as a light bomber Squadron R. Auxiliary A.F. equipped with Hawker Harts/Hinds in 1936.

December 1938 - September 1939: Yeadon. Hawker Hinds.
Hinds Serial No.
K5421, K5451, K5469, K5497, K5519, K5542, K6728, 6730, 6790, 6820, 6846, K6850, L7177, L7185, L7188.

September 1939: Yeadon. Spitfire Mk 1
September 1939 - October 1939: Catterick. Spitfire Mk 1
Spitfire Serial No.
L1058, 1086, 1064, 1071, R4173, 6631, 6979, R6906, 6915, P9425, R6706, N3024, X4587.

October 1939: Acklington. Spitfire 1s moved to Manston.
31 July 1946: Reformed at Yeadon as a R. Auxiliary A.F. Squadron equipped with D.H. Mosquito NF30 (1946-1948).
Serial No.
NT283, 334, 422, NT449, 568 NT615, TA341, VA883, VA926.
Vickers Supermarine Spitfire LF 16e (1948-1950)
Serial No.
TE478, 477, 463, 347, 302, 338 RW359, 378, 381, 382 SL561, 719, SM316 TB911

October 1950-1957: Church Fenton. Spitfire LF 16e (1950-1951).

October 1950-1957: Church Fenton. Gloster Meteor F8 (1951-1957)
1957: Yeadon. Disbanded.

A Spitfire LF 16e RAP-F parked
outside a Bellman hangar at Yeadon.

Vickers Supermarine Spitfire LF 16e.
(1948-50).

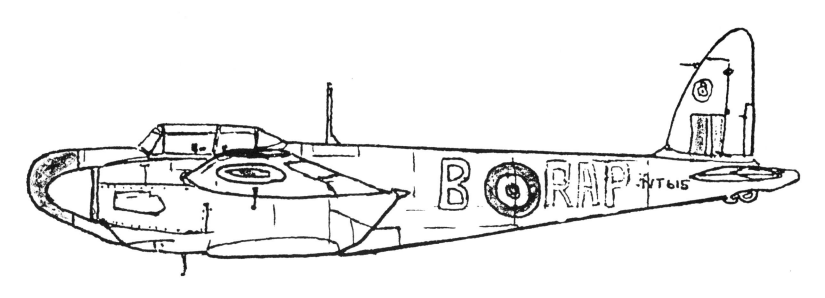

De Havilland Mosquito N.F.30.
(1946-48).

*One of the Squadron's Spitfire 16 on display
at Church Fenton.*